# SERENITY *TO GO*

## *CALMING TECHNIQUES FOR YOUR HECTIC LIFE*

*To Sharon*
*for a serene*
*future*
*Mina Hamilton*

**Mina Hamilton**

*NEW HARBINGER PUBLICATIONS, INC.*

## Publisher's Note

*This publication is designed to provide accurate and authoritative information in regard to the subject matter covered. It is sold with the understanding that the publisher is not engaged in rendering psychological, financial, legal, or other professional services. If expert assistance or counseling is needed, the services of a competent professional should be sought.*

Distributed in the U.S.A. by Publishers Group West; in Canada by Raincoast Books; in Great Britain by Airlift Book Company, Ltd.; in South Africa by Real Books, Ltd.; in Australia by Boobook; and in New Zealand by Tandem Press.

Copyright © 2001 by Mina Hamilton
        New Harbinger Publications, Inc.
        5674 Shattuck Avenue
        Oakland, CA 94609

Cover design by Poulson/Gluck Designs
Cover illustration by Jonathan Evans/Artville
Edited by Heather Garnos
Book design by Michele Waters

ISBN 1-57224-235-3 Paperback

New Harbinger Publications' Web site address:
www.newharbinger.com

03    02    01

10   9   8   7   6   5   4   3   2   1

First printing

To Abby
Whose love and support were vital

# Contents

## Wake-up Call 27

## Commuter Special: By Car and by Train 43

## Nine to Five (Including Lunch) 75

## Rush-Hour Relief: By Bus, Subway, and Foot 105

## Home at Last                                        137

# Acknowledgments

Many wonderful individuals have made this book possible. Toni Packer, Rick Jarow, Joanna Macy, Ram Dass, and Thich Nhat Hanh have all been my inspiration. Over many years at retreats and workshops, I have absorbed a modest amount of their deep wisdom and insight. Without these teachers, *Serenity to Go* would not have come into existence. In addition, key to the conceptualization of this book have been my many students and clients in stress-reduction, relaxation, and yoga classes. Working with and learning from these students has been and continues to be profoundly inspiring. Since I first started to study stress reduction and yoga thirteen years ago, countless teachers at the Kripalu Center for Yoga and Health have contributed to my understanding of how to be present and calm in life's difficult moments. In particular, I wish to thank Todd Norian and Karen Kaumudi Hasskarl. In addition my gratitude to Dr. Jeffrey Migdow, Adrienne Jamiel, and Irene Dowd, my wise teachers of anatomy and physiology. Thanks to my editor at New Harbinger, Heather Garnos, for her astute editorial skill and to June Peoples, Adrienne Jamiel, Abby Turner, and Katherine Boyle who spent many hours reading and editing the manuscript and encouraging the author. Finally, my appreciation to Terry Cramer, and my sister, Lisa Hamilton. Their support was invaluable.

# Welcome to
## *Serenity to Go*

# For the Journey:
# What to Bring with You

Whether your gut is churning in yet another traffic jam or you're ready to "kill" while standing in line at the supermarket, it's the premise of *Serenity to Go* that it's in your power to transform these moments. You can be serene in the most unlikely of times. The times you previously thought of as times to be gotten *through* as quickly as possible. The "I-can't-stand-this-a-moment-longer" times.

Sounds pretty Pollyanna, doesn't it? Stick with me for a few pages before saying, "Impossible." I'm going to ask you to see the "in-between" as a rich, fertile place—a place ripe with opportunity. Using the simple, calming techniques in these pages, you'll learn to change your experience of the "in-betweens" so they become a place of calmness and serenity, a place of interest and, quite possibly, beauty. You'll also learn to transform irritating moments into neutral, ho-hum moments. Or even curious and funny moments.

Probably you're already feeling a tad anxious. "What is she going to ask me to do? Or give up?" Relax. You don't have to buy fancy equipment, nor do you have to don a white turban and sit in the lotus position. You don't have to stand on your head or twist yourself into the shape of a pretzel. You don't even have to give up chocolate or cappuccino.

There is, however, one thing you need for this journey: an open mind. You may retort, "I have a wonderfully, gloriously open mind." I know you do. But perhaps you can tweak it so it's even *more* open. Let's look more closely for a second at what *is* an open mind.

For one, an open mind means a willingness to experiment. To try something new, even if it initially strikes you as silly or stupid. (Those judgments may be defenses you cook up to stop yourself from experimenting.) It also means a willingness to re-examine, to look freshly at some of your age-old thoughts and, if need be, toss them out! Like a gray whale whose skin is encrusted with barnacles, you're loaded with habits. I'm not getting personal—we all have them. You, me, everyone loves habits. We're hooked. They're familiar. They're comfortable, even when they're quite out-of-date.

You have set ways of responding to all kinds of stimuli in your life. Hmmm. Remember, an open mind? A mind willing to experiment? *Serenity to Go* will give you the simple tools to enable you to react differently—or not react at all. In short, to create some new habits. You may not have given a thought to the consequences of the old ones, yet you'll soon realize that the new habits make you feel better. Less stressed. More calm.

Let's look at a moment that you probably hate, and that you encounter too often. For example, someone leaning, *really* leaning, on the horn of his or her automobile. Whether you're standing on the sidewalk bearing a clump of lilac blossoms for your sweetheart or slumped in your car waiting for the gridlock to unlock, the sound irritates you. With no say-so from your conscious mind, thoughts are rushing into your head, such as, "That jerk, why doesn't he shut up?" "What an idiot!" "I hate inconsiderate drivers."

This set of thoughts pops into your mind whenever you hear the irritating horn sound. The thoughts are so familiar, so automatic, you're hardly aware of them. But they actually have a profound impact on your life. You start getting angry. As a result, your body gets into the act. Your heart pounds, your blood pressure goes up, stress chemicals flood your system. You're physiologically ready to punch someone in the nose.

You may protest, "What do you mean, the thoughts are making me madder than a hornet? It's the rude *driver*." Well, it is the driver, but it's also you and how you're responding. What if you were to simply take some long, deep breaths? What if you were to not respond? If you were to look up at the sky and enjoy a gorgeous bank of billowing clouds? The person is still leaning on his horn, but it doesn't *get* you. You have made a choice to redefine the situation. I know, I know. This isn't easy. That's why you need some gentle coaching. You're going to have to *practice* our calming techniques. It's not as if, presto, overnight your life will completely change. (I wish I could promise you that, but it wouldn't be honest or fair.)

What are some of the additional characteristics of an open mind? An open mind is also a flexible one. It looks at a situation from several different angles. It is willing—perhaps grumpily, perhaps grudgingly—to admit, "Hey, *my* viewpoint is not necessarily the *right* one." An open mind can say, "Hey, that 'jerk' isn't a jerk after all. He just made an honest mistake. It was an accident." An open mind might admit, "Ah yes, I've made the identical mistake."

Definitely a sense of humor is recommended for this journey. We'll do some things in this book that may initially make you feel anxious. Though most of the calming techniques described here can be done inconspicuously, sometimes you may feel awkward. For example, you're going to stretch in odd places.

In the twenty-first century people run through the streets dressed in the scantiest of costumes: for example, a purple jogging bra and shorts that barely cover the tushy. Before the jogging craze, which erupted in the 1970s, appearing half-naked in the best neighborhoods—from Park Avenue to Pasadena—would have been considered beyond the pale. Nowadays you either do it yourself or don't bat an eye when someone else does it.

Perhaps waiting in line at the post office is going to be your new venue for stretching. Or a crowded bus or train might be the spot. Although the *Serenity to Go* exercises for public places are mostly extremely subtle and basically invisible, you may at times *feel* conspicuous, even if you're not. Go ahead, take the risk. Why not become a trendsetter, just like those joggers back in the 1970s.

You're also going to consciously breathe at unexpected moments. Even the perfectly natural, biologically necessary act of breathing can make us feel vulnerable. Maybe someone will hear us or notice us? Hey, everyone around you is gabbing on a cell phone, listening to CDs, or nodding out—and you don't dare breathe?

Every time your resistance kicks in with one of these objections, you might ask yourself, "Is this an example of an open mind or is it an old way of thinking?" "Am I stuck in a twentieth-century way of thinking?" "How can I coax, nudge, charm myself into a fresh way that's more consonant with the bright new millennium?"

So what are the tools that will allow you to transform this moment? For the answer to this question, turn to "Recipe for Finding the Calm" on page 7.

Think you're too cranky, too set in your ways, too old to change? Please note: New scientific data says that even as an adult you continue growing *new* brain cells in your memory retrieval center, the hippocampus. Even if you've flown past thirty, you can teach your brain new tricks. Why not go for it?

## The Recipe for Finding the Calm: Five Ingredients

This book is a bit like a cookbook: You read the recipe for the occasion at hand. You'll dip in and out of sections depending upon your mood and activity. Exercises are situation specific. Traffic jam gets your goat? Turn to page 43, "Commuter Special." Need to be calmer at the office? Check out page 75, "Nine to Five."

We recommend you *carry* this book with you. The calming techniques are all very simple and easy. In the heat of the moment, however, you may forget what you read back in the security of your cozy home.

*Serenity to Go* is going to coach you in five techniques to help you be serene: Stretching. Breathing. Practicing compassion. Being grateful. Becoming aware—in a fresh, new, playful way—of the wonders of the flora and fauna, including humans, that surround you.

Just the word, "stretching," may turn some folks off. Not to worry. *Anybody* can do these stretches. Couch potatoes, exercise phobics, jogging enthusiasts, or yoga adepts. Even people in wheelchairs can do many of them.

You'll be stretching and breathing in the most unlikely of places: at the post office, on a bus, even stuck in traffic. Generally these stretches are inconspicuous. Even someone standing right next to you on the subway will not bat an eye.

The key to the calming effect of these stretches is *how* you do them. Forget the gym mentality where you step on a treadmill and watch TV. Sweat pours off your brow. Your legs and arms pump. Your muscles are at the max, straining, pushing, trembling. In contrast, the stretches here are subtle.

It's about being gentle and soft. It's not about trying to jam your body into the straitjacket of what you, Madison Avenue, or Hollywood thinks you *ought* to look like. It's not about trying to do something perfectly. It's about "easy does it."

Another key difference between a gym mentality and the stretches in this book? The location of your mind. At a gym it may be off frolicking in the waves of an island in the South Pacific or whatever else is beckoning from the TV screen. Or while jogging you may be thinking about the tofu burgers you're planning for supper.

I will gently encourage your lively mind to return from its perpetual wandering. Its constant worrying about the future, the rehashing of the past, the nonstop planning, scheming, dreaming. As you stretch, I'll coach you to return to an awareness of your body in this moment. "Ah yes, I have a neck and I'm going to notice what's going on with it." I'll coach you to become aware of the physical sensations of the stretch.

At the same time you'll learn to observe the lightning fast, rat-tat-tat thoughts coursing through your brain *as* you stretch. Most of us carry around a horde of nasty judgments about our bodies. We drag out these negative thoughts at the slightest provocation, and for many people even a gentle stretch is a provocation.

We'll practice observing these judgments and then letting them go. What does "letting" go of a thought mean? It means not attaching to a thought, not following it down the path of self-criticism and recrimination. For example, in the midst of a *Serenity to Go* stretch the thought might be, "I need to tone my stomach muscles." If you attach to the thought, you'll start an old tape. "I'm too fat." "Why did I eat that piece of chocolate cream pie today?" Yadda-yadda.

When you practice detachment or let go of the thought, you neutrally notice it, "Ah, there I go again worrying about my abs," and then you refocus your attention on your breathing.

"Breathe." "Take long, deep breaths." "Full, relaxed breaths." You'll see these phrases repeatedly. Breathing helps to bring us back to an awareness of what's happening in this moment.

By what's happening I don't mean the *external* phenomena of a traffic jam. Although you may not like to admit it, generally, you can't change the external reality. Apparently, the cars are stacked up from here to the North Pole. You can't board Harry Potter's Nimbus 2000 and soar over the sea of cars. You can't pave over the United States or instantly create a new public transportation system. Nor, much as you yearn to, can you find a secret, uncrowded detour.

What you can do is change your *internal* reaction—by first noticing how you're breathing. Just quietly observing the breath without any intention to change it can be calming. Or you can notice the quality of your breath; whether you're breathing shallowly or deeply. Then you have a *choice*. You can shift the breath into a slower, deeper, *calming* rhythm. It's so simple, it seems almost like magic. The trick, of course, is remembering both to notice the breath and then to let it deepen. *Serenity to Go* will regularly coach you in this skill.

Another key ingredient in finding the calm? Compassion exercises. These are gentle reminders that there is another way of looking at the situation you're up in arms about. So often you're single-mindedly focused on "my hurt" or "my pain." And your experience of a situation is made considerably worse by your attitude toward the people around you. "He stepped on my toe." "She cut in front of me." You're off and running, so consumed with blame, frustration, irritation, anger, that your body is flooded with adrenaline, your heart races, your blood pressure spikes. If you were a dog, you'd be growling and baring your teeth.

But we aren't dogs. We have a *choice* to be different in these pesky situations. We can see the people around us not as competitors, not as stealing our slowly moving parking spot on the interstate highway, but as folk we have oodles in common with. As fellow human beings, vulnerable, lovable (to somebody), doing the best they can. As soon as we start thinking about the feelings and experiences we *share* with the people around us, presto, the dynamics change.

"But I'm a very compassionate person," you vehemently protest. "I don't need any exercises." Of course you're compassionate. Deeply and profoundly so. But I'll eat my hat if you don't need a little friendly encouragement on how to be *more* compassionate while sitting in a traffic jam or packed in, cheek-by-jowl, with hundreds of rush-hour commuters.

I'll also offer tips on how to feel grateful—just at the moment when you feel stressed. In your single-minded focus on your problems, the problems often swell up way out of proportion to what's really going on. Let's face it, you often forget the basics: the amazing gifts inside your own body and right before your eyes. *Serenity to Go,* without being saccharine or sentimental, will give you practice in appreciating the ordinary things you often take for granted. The ordinary things that are, in fact, *extraordinary,* like your heart thumping away through the night or the tuna-fish-on-rye sandwich sitting on your plate.

Finally, there are simple techniques to help you to become more aware of the universe around you, to see your world more freshly. From a new perspective. We're all plagued by "been there, done that-itis." And if we're bored, boy, are we more prone to anger, irritation, and stress! That's why I'll gently and humorously nudge you to feel your relationship to the earth beneath you, the sky above, and the unexpected pleasures in between. So often we are in such a hurry, so fixated on getting "there," that we miss the wondrous, beautiful, silly, curious, interesting—and funny—universe of people and things all around us. Playfulness is a key ingredient here because there's enough serious stuff in your life already.

So get ready to be serene.

## Are You Breathing? Practical Tips

Of course you're *already* breathing! By breathe, I mean, deep, diaphragmatic or "belly" breathing. Not shallow, chest breathing. Which way are you breathing right now? A major clue is what's happening with your belly. Become aware of it. If it's relaxed, gently expanding in and out, you're breathing diaphragmatically. On the other hand, if your belly is tight, your shoulders are hiked up, and you feel tense, you're breathing shallowly.

Why bother to change how you breathe? You've made it this far without deep breathing, so why start now? There's one whopper of a reason: Deep breathing activates physiological processes in your body that are sometimes called the relaxation response. This response includes a host of complex neurological and biochemical factors. The bottom line? When you breathe diaphragmatically (sometimes this form of breathing is also called "abdominal" breathing), your body goes into a rest phase. Physiologically you start to relax. And guess what? When you relax physically, your emotions start to quiet down too. Seems pretty obvious, doesn't it? What's not so obvious is that you can control this reaction *voluntarily* by the way you breathe.

Let's check again how you're breathing right now. Is your belly soft, slowly expanding in and out? Did I say "soft"? Yes, I know it's heresy. We live in a culture that worships flat, hard bellies. If you can't get one via the treadmill, cinch or suck it in. Even to speak the word "belly" is subversive in certain quarters, but let's temporarily unshackle ourselves from the dictates of Madison Avenue.

Experiment with relaxing your belly. Try this first in the privacy of your own home. You'll start by lying down on the floor. Do not do this on the bed. (You won't get enough support for your back.) Place an exercise or camping mat on the floor, or go for some folded blankets to give yourself some cushioning. Most people will prefer to lie with their back on the floor and a pillow placed underneath the knees. This helps relax the lower back. If the pillow is too small, the lower back will arch, causing back strain. A good-sized pillow to use is a standard bed pillow. Add extra pillows until your back is comfy.

Guess what? Everybody's back is unique. Yours is no exception. You may be among those who actually feel more comfortable with their legs stretched out straight onto the floor. Make adjustments and shifts until you find the position that *works* for your body.

Next, relax your shoulders. Let go of the burdens you're carrying around in your shoulders. Relax and soften the muscles in the back, letting those muscles sink toward the floor. Now, place your hands on your stomach. Start letting the breath go down into the stomach. Feel your belly rising and falling.

At first this may seem difficult. The chest rises and falls, but your belly doesn't budge. Check to see if your waistband or belt is too tight. Undo the top button or release the belt a notch. To help yourself get the feel of it, place a large book on your belly. (Go for a tome like *Webster's Collegiate Dictionary*.) Notice how the book rises and falls with your breath.

Let the inhalation and exhalation be slow and steady. Notice if you're trying too hard. Are you pushing or struggling? Back off. Let yourself be gentle. Do this form of breathing for three to five minutes.

After you have done this breathing for a couple of minutes, remove the book and see if you can feel your belly rising and falling without the weight of Webster's lexicon. If not, go back to using the book.

The first couple of times, be sure you do this exercise when your roommates are out, children are occupied, spouse is asleep. No need to subject yourself to curious glances or derisive remarks. If anybody asks what are you doing, calmly say, "I'm relaxing."

Why do I call this "belly" breathing? Everybody knows we breathe with the lungs, not the stomach! This is technically true, but during deep breathing, the belly does move in and out. A bit of an anatomy lesson might help to clarify why.

The diaphragm is a sheath of muscle attached to the bottom edge of the ribs, front and back. It separates the chest or lung cavity from the abdominal cavity. This muscle can rise and fall. If the muscles pulls downward, it creates extra space in the chest cavity, allowing the lungs to expand more freely, to be more fully filled with oxygen. At the same time the downward motion causes the contents of the abdominal cavity to bulge outward slightly.

On the inhalation, the belly balloons out. On the exhalation, it sinks down. When you first practice belly breathing, it can feel awkward. This is because we've forgotten how to breathe in this perfectly natural way. Yet it's something we did automatically as infants. Next time you're diapering your adorable niece, notice how her belly moves in and out as she breathes. Meanwhile, her shoulders and chest remain relatively still. That's what we want to relearn to do as adults.

Please note: Technically speaking, you're never breathing *only* with the diaphragm. As you've just noticed with your niece or another child, there will always also be some involvement of the chest. By diaphragmatic breathing we mean a breathing technique in which "belly" breathing predominates.

Deep breathing is a skill that you won't necessarily learn overnight. You will have to practice. Luckily it's something you can practice *anywhere*. Once you've done it on the floor a couple of times, start doing the same type of breathing while waiting for the bus, standing in line at the post office, or stalled in traffic. In the case of the traffic jam, be sure to roll up your windows and turn on the air-conditioning so you don't inhale extra carbon monoxide. Even small amounts of this invisible and odorless substance can cause headaches, decreased alertness, and drowsiness.

Are you into athletics? Running? Cycling? Swimming? Then you're already familiar with diaphragmatic breathing. Remember that during these activities you're wearing an elastic waistband or expandable spandex. Your belly has space to move. You wouldn't dream of running a marathon with a leather belt cinched up tight around your waist. You'd probably pass out before mile three. Well, your life is a marathon. Give yourself a break. Loosen your belt. Start breathing. Long, slow, and steady.

esc

# Quick Anatomy Lesson:
# Why Deep Breathing Helps

You'll be doing a lot of different calming techniques in *Serenity to Go*. A vital component of them all? Deep breathing. Slow and steady. This form of breathing is so important, we're going to give you a few extra facts as to *why* it's going to add to your serenity levels. So even if anatomy and physiology aren't normally your cup of tea, read on.

Deep or diaphragmatic breathing enhances the relaxation response, which is basically the opposite of the fight or flight response, which is what happens when your body gets ready to respond to an emergency, such as an out-of-control car veering in your direction. In that case your body gets ready to leap to safety; your respiratory rate jumps (as in short gasps), your heart rate increases, your blood pressure zips up, and your system is flooded with adrenaline and other stress hormones. Your pupils dilate (so you can see better), and your sweat glands spring into action (that's why you literally get hot under the collar). It's a highly desirable response for a true emergency (the veering car).

In the relaxation response, your physiological system does almost the exact opposite of the fight or flight response. Your respiratory rate slows, heart slows, blood pressure dips, pupils contract, you sweat less. In short, your body comes out of emergency mode. You start calming down.

What's astounding is that you can at will initiate this calming response by changing your breathing pattern. It's because the act of breathing has a very special property. Normally we all breathe unconsciously. No matter what we're doing, sleeping like a log or dancing up a storm, our lungs suck oxygen in and pump carbon dioxide out. It's what anatomy books call an automatic function. Just the way the heart, with no say-so from us, keeps the blood briskly circulating or the liver squirts out enzymes, the lungs automatically do their inhale-exhale thing. The oddity is that although we breathe automatically, we can also control the breath. Hence we can hold our breath as we dive underwater to look at a coral fish or slow it down to deliver that high note in chorus. And we can change the *quality* of our breath, as in slowing it down, to help ourselves be more serene in the midst of what a moment before was a "crisis."

Let's experiment for a moment with the quality of your breath. I'm not talking about mouthwash! But the tempo, the rhythm, the feeling (rushed or slow) of the breath. Either seated or lying down, deliberately decide to take in quick, ragged, shallow gasps of breath. (If you have asthma or emphysema, or are subject to panic attacks, please skip this exercise.) In short order, you'll start feeling anxious, hyper. Probably you'll notice your chest and shoulders becoming quite active. Please don't do these fast, rapid breaths for more than a few seconds. You might get dizzy.

Now return to more normal breathing. To a longer, steadier breath. A fuller, more relaxed breath. A deeper, abdominal breath. Even if you don't yet have the knack of diaphragmatic breathing (you'll probably need more practice), almost immediately you will feel calmer. You'll note how quickly the body responds to a different way of breathing. Pretty amazing! Of course the skill is learning to do deep breathing regularly throughout your day—and in crises, a skill *Serenity to Go* will be teaching you.

The other advantage of deep breathing? It improves the *efficiency* with which we breathe. It works like this: As you breathe, oxygen enters the lungs and travels into millions of alveoli, or tiny air sacs. These delicate membranes are surrounded by a myriad of blood vessels. Here oxygen is transferred to the bloodstream. The arteries zip the oxygen out to brain, muscles, nerves, and internal organs, fueling a host of vital functions.

If you're breathing shallowly, the flow of air, including that nifty oxygen, tends to concentrate in the top two-thirds of the lungs. This area is less blood rich than the lower part. Therefore, when breathing shallowly, you have to breathe more rapidly to get the proper amount of oxygen out into the body. This means the lungs and heart have to work *harder* than would be the case if you were breathing deeply. The result: Your pulse rate goes up and even your blood pressure rises. Maintain this pattern of breathing over time? You'll start feeling both anxious and tired.

But breathe deep into the lungs, and there's a rich concentration of blood waiting to transport the oxygen out to the far corners of the body. In this case, your heart beats much more slowly to send out an *equal* amount of oxygen. The rate of your pulse slows down, and your blood pressure decreases. Presto: less strain on the heart and less fatigue for you.

Another way to look at this? The number of breaths you have to take *per minute* and *per day* when chest breathing is predominant, versus when diaphragmatic breathing predominates. In the first case, sixteen to twenty breaths a minute or 22,000 to 25,000 breaths per day. In the second case, six to eight breaths per minute, 10,000 to 12,000 per day. With chest breathing you are working *twice* as hard to achieve the same result! That's a heck of a lot of extra and unnecessary work.

Another key factor: In shallow breathing, you negatively affect the balance of gases in your bloodstream. You're inefficiently cleansing the body of the waste product, carbon dioxide. Excess carbon dioxide in the bloodstream can adversely affect the blood's acidity. The result? You feel fatigued and nervous. Shorthand: You feel stressed.

All of these are great reasons to breathe deeply. The best reason? You *feel* better.

esc

# The Egyptian Pose:
# Home Base for Tranquillity

This is your home base for many of the calming techniques in *Serenity to Go*. It's supremely easy, a no-brainer. Whether you're physically challenged with a daunting case of scoliosis or as sleek and fit as a gazelle on the African plain, the Egyptian Pose is for you. Named after those stolid, solid blocks of stone from ancient Egypt that have been successfully staring down tourists and museumgoers for centuries, it's unforgettable and timeless.

You'll do it in the most unlikely places. Sitting in a traffic jam, staring at your computer, jostling elbows with fellow commuters on a train, or munching down a sandwich at your favorite coffee shop.

Let's say you're going to do your first session of the Egyptian Pose on the 7:02 A.M. commuter train. (If you don't commute by train, substitute an alternate mode of transportation.) On this particular morning, leave your home five minutes early. Do some prepping before you hit the station. Otherwise, as soon as you see the gleam of the tracks, you'll forget your good intentions and be swept up in your flaring-at-the-nostrils racehorse-on-amphetamine habits.

Once you've parked your car, walk a tad slower than usual. Notice your breath. Let it deepen. Look up. Examine the clouds, enjoy the sun. Glance around you. Observe something that you've never noticed before: the way a shaft of light turns the finials on a wrought-iron fence golden. The leer on the corner church's gargoyles. A flower box crammed with marigolds.

Okay. Here's the station entrance. See the other commuters running, loping, galloping toward the platform?

Ignore them. You're walking to a different drummer. It doesn't matter how fast they're moving. You're oblivious, committed to maintaining your turtlelike pace.

Continue to walk slowly. Are your fellow commuters nipping at your heels, cursing and muttering? Politely let them pass you. Resist the temptation to run—and oh, what a temptation!

Once on the train, forego your usual whipping out of the newspaper. Find a seat. (If you can't locate a seat, turn to "Rush-Hour Relief," page 105.) Now get ready for the Egyptian Pose. Position yourself in one of two ways: Either start sitting with your buttocks far back in the seat and your back gently pressed against the back of the seat, or sit with your buttocks about midway into the seat and with your back not touching the seat back. Select the position that feels most comfortable for you.

Place each foot firmly on the floor with your feet directly underneath your knees. Gently rest your hands on your knees. If you're a woman carrying a pocketbook, place the pocketbook on your lap and rest your hands on top of the pocketbook. If you're carrying a briefcase, rest it on your knees or place it between your feet.

Close your eyes. Or, if you feel too vulnerable closing them, keep them open, but with a soft, unfocused gaze. Avoid making eye contact with anyone. Avoid observing the details of your fellow passengers. Start taking deep breaths. Feel the breath going right down into the belly. Let the breath out with a sigh. Don't worry—nobody will hear you over the din.

Feel your butt in contact with the seat. This is often a hard one for women because of unreasonable dictates of fashion calling for hard-as-steel buns. See if you can avoid making any judgments about the size or fleshiness of your butt. I know this is tough, but guess what? You'd be in a terrific fix without that padding. You'd be in agony, teetering on the little bony protrusions at the bottom of your pelvis. In fact, you wouldn't be able to sit comfortably at all! So give your butt a break and simply notice your highly useful buttocks touching the seat.

Become aware of the top, or crown, of your head. Allow the head to gently lift upward at that place, the spinal column gently elongating. Throughout this guide we use the term "elongate" to encourage you to lift *without* going into ramrod-straight, military posture. Your back naturally has curves; as you lengthen the spine upward, enjoy those curves. Allow the jaw muscles to soften. Check out your neck. Is it relaxed?

Resist the temptation to cross your legs! Lightly press down with your feet. Press down with the heels, balls, and toes. See if you can feel the floor through your shoes. Notice if there is more weight on one foot than on the other. Make any necessary adjustments to equalize the weight.

On the next inhalation, notice the subtle movement in your torso. The spine lifts slightly. If you feel the shoulders also start to lift, let them drop down. On the exhalation, feel how the torso sinks down. Continue to observe the breath. Instead of sitting rigid, let your body sway with the motion of the train. Allow a sense of softness, of flexibility to come into the spine.

If you're sitting with your back against the seat, gently press your shoulder blades toward the seat behind you. Continue deep breathing. Relax the facial muscles. Let the muscles on the forehead, around the eyes, around the mouth become soft.

Bring to mind the image of the Sphinx: unflappable, inscrutable. Unknowable riddles course through your body; centuries fly. After a little practice, you'll start to feel a shift deep inside you. You'll start feeling as rock-solid, as calm as the red granite statues of Queen Hatshepsut waiting out the centuries at the Metropolitan Museum of Art in New York. One of the first queens of Egypt, her statue's been hanging around since 1500 B.C.

Gradually, you'll start having astounding moments when you're only vaguely aware of the petty coming and going of humanity. You'll be unperturbed by your fellow commuters. You may even start imagining you can hear the Nile lapping at your feet, the sharp slap of the sails of an occasional *dhow*. Do not expect the fruits of the Egyptian Pose to spring upon you suddenly. Like any worthwhile skill, this one takes time, persistence, and a healthy sense of humor.

Congratulations! You're ready to dive into the soothing world of *Serenity to Go*.

# Medical Advisory:
# Moderation Is the Best Policy

Many of the calming techniques described in *Serenity to Go* are mental exercises that anybody and everybody can do just about anywhere. The physical stretches in this book are easy and safe. Whether you're a type-A jock and fit as the proverbial fiddle or sixty-five and decidedly creaky, there's something here for you.

One can, however, do too much of a good thing. Please do not do a stretch to the point of pain. Stay within your comfort zone. In some gyms there's an unfortunate adherence to the "no pain, no gain" theory of exercise. Please dispense with this viewpoint. If you hold a stretch and are in pain, your body is sending you an important message. Back off. Stretch a little less, or come out entirely. Always adapt a stretch so it works for you. Grinning and bearing it may result in hurting yourself.

You have high blood pressure and are currently on medication? You can do absolutely *everything* in this book. Faithful followers of *Serenity to Go* may find themselves becoming generally calmer in their everyday life. You might even find that your blood pressure may actually decrease, in which case you might need to reduce the dose of your medication. Adjust your medication only in consultation with your health care practitioner.

There are a few precautions that people with specific medical conditions should follow.

You have high blood pressure and are *not* on medication? Do *not* do any of the stretches that involve bending forward to the extent that your head is below the level of your heart. For example, the forward bend in "Caffeine Substitute" on page 76 is not for you.

If you have diabetes, whether you are on medication or not, do not do *any* forward bends that result in your head being below your heart. The same precaution applies to persons with retinal problems, glaucoma, hernias, or heart problems.

Suffer from back pain? The situation is more complex. As you know, chronic, low-grade lower-back pain isn't fun. It may make you understandably fearful of doing any stretches. Yet stretches may be exactly what you need. *When in doubt as to what is the best course of action for your back, consult with a doctor or health care practitioner.*

Often back pain is an indicator that you're suffering from poor body mechanics. For example, you may repeatedly lift things with a rounded back and straight knees. Or those aches may signal poor alignment, such as from sitting crouched over a computer all day. Moderate stretches for the back can be marvelously healing for stressed backs.

Sometimes acute back pain is caused by muscle spasm. After the initial episode of acute pain has passed, resuming your regular routine—including gentle exercise—is generally considered the best treatment. If you exercise gently and regularly, you probably will have fewer episodes. Please note: Gentle exercise does not include playing fiercely competitive tennis, biking fifty miles at a stretch, or running in a marathon. Much as you love these activities they may not be good for your back.

Each person's back is unique. Discover what *works* for yours. Your back pain is the result of an injury? Been lifting boulders in your new rock garden or moving the grand piano? Or perhaps you have a disk problem? A disk that may be impinging on a nerve? Certain exercises may be con-traindicated. Again, *consult your health care practitioner.*

Had recent surgery? Please seek professional medical advice.

# Wake-up Call

# When the Alarm Goes Off:
## "Hey, I'm Alive"

Perhaps the most amazing event of the day is waking up. You survived! Throughout the night, with absolutely no effort on your part, all systems were A-OK.

Your heart kept beating. Your lungs inflated and deflated, delivering just the perfect amount of oxygen to your bloodstream. Your bone marrow cranked out red and white blood cells. Your brain sent tiny electrochemical messages to your nerves. Each and every one of your trillions of cells was a virtual furnace of activity with nutrients efficiently sucked in and waste products neatly ejected. This list of activities represents a tiny percentage of the amazing, complex, and subtle events that occurred while you were in slumber land.

It's easy to complain about the things that have gone wrong, hard to remind ourselves of what we take for granted. "Hey, I'm Alive" gives you an opportunity to correct that imbalance. Of course, how you choose to begin your morning will have an impact on how you feel during the rest of the day. Not to worry—you don't have to pump iron or do push-ups. All you're going to do is practice the art of giving thanks. But you do need to prepare the night before.

Set your alarm two to three minutes earlier. Make an intention to have some quiet time. If, while still half asleep, you usually check out the traffic advisories, forget it. Decide now to turn off the radio the minute the alarm goes off. If you're in the habit of clicking on the TV before your eyelids are pried open, resist the temptation. Catch the weatherman later.

Alert your spouse or partner. Tomorrow—for a few minutes—you're foregoing chatting. Someone's car alarm drives you nuts at 3:00 A.M.? So be it. Save your complaints till breakfast.

Decide the night before where you're going to do this exercise. You can do it while still lying in bed. In the shower is a possibility; so is sitting on a chair in your bedroom, or sitting on your bed. (Forget the living room or at breakfast if you have roommates, children, or other members of your household who might interrupt you.)

Depending upon your usual level of grogginess, you may want to go into the bathroom and douse your face with cold water before returning to the place where you have decided to do this meditation. You might want to practice first on a weekend when you have more time. After you have done it a few times on a weekend, then go for a weekday.

Although many wondrous events happen in your body during the night, plan to focus on the heart. For starters, take several long, deep breaths. If you're sitting in a chair, gently elongate the spine and relax the shoulders. If you're lying in bed, lie in a comfortable position with your lower back supported. Sometimes it's nice to lie on your back with a pillow tucked underneath your knees. Find the position that is most comfortable for you.

Review some of your heart's accomplishments. Your heart kept beating, all through the night. This tough hunk of muscle—the strongest muscle in the body—has this astounding property. Through thick and thin, it keeps on beating.

Whether you're rollerblading in the park or snoozing at the opera, your heart delivers the goods. Whether you're grabbing a thrift shop bargain or eating caviar, this bundle of energy is at work. Ditto at night. Whether you were dreaming about a vacation in Bali or had a nightmare about your ex, your heart faithfully, doggedly went about its business, steady as a metronome. With no conscious help from you: pump, pump, pump.

Think about and appreciate the properties of this marvelous piece of your anatomy. This small organ weighs about one pound and is customarily described as being about the size of a clenched fist. This description is a tad aggressive for my taste. It's also the size of a baseball or an orange. (Of course, your heart's size varies according to your overall size.) It's remarkably strong. It processes about 2,000 gallons of blood a day.

It's amazing. This muscle keeps on pushing blood up to your brain and out to every bone, muscle, and organ. As a result, a steady supply of nifty little packets of oxygen and nutrients is delivered to the trillions of cells throughout your body. If you slept eight hours last night, your heart beat about 29,000 times. If you are now 32, your heart will have beaten over 1 billion times.

Your heart speeds up when you run up the stairs, slows down when you catnap. It can turn over or leap when your sweetheart appears at the door. It's steadfast, reliable, your closest friend.

Take some long, deep breaths. Give your heart some metaphoric pats on the back. Your heart deserves high kudos. Whatever daunting tasks await you today, whatever challenges are coming your way, thank your heart. It did its job last night. Take another moment to lavish more praise on the flawless performance of this superb organ.

Hey, you're fully, gloriously alive. What a gift.

## In the Shower: Gentle—and Safe—Stretch for the Spine

Do you wake up feeling lithe as a panther? Or do you find yourself remarkably similar to the Wizard of Oz's tin man—decidedly creaky and in need of oil? Either way, treat your back to a stretch while you're in the shower. Convinced you don't have time? I know you're raring to go, ready to go out and slay dragons. Rest assured this sequence takes three minutes, max. And it's worth it! There's nothing like a wide-awake, flexible spine to make you feel alive and energetic.

Caution: You're stepping into an enamel bathtub? Before embarking on this exercise, be sure you have a rubber mat on the floor of the tub. This is the only piece of equipment required for readers of *Serenity to Go*. Don't own a rubber mat? *Do not proceed with this stretch until you have bought one.*

Since the book isn't waterproof and you can't carry it into the shower, read this sequence before stepping into the shower. Please be sure not to do the exercises until you have doused your back with warm water!

Go ahead with whatever are your morning ablutions. Washing, shampooing, singing. Then turn your back to that wonderful spray of warm water. For a few moments let the heat of the water wake up your sleepy spine. Enjoy the spray soothing the muscles of your back.

Now for some easy stretches. Stand with both feet firmly on the floor of the tub or shower. Place your feet about hip width apart with the toes pointing forward. Let your arms hang by your sides. Now allow the spine to elongate. As you lengthen upward, keep your shoulders relaxed.

Next do a gentle side arc. I said, "Gentle." Gentle means slowly—as if you had all the time in the world. It also means *no* pushing or forcing.

Are you someone who dives into the middle of a book? Invariably skips introductions? State secret: So am I. Please do yourself a favor and return to "Recipe for Finding the Calm" on page 7 and read *how* to stretch. The stretches in this book are designed to be done in a certain way. Rush through them, and guess what? You'll get stressed out, exactly the opposite goal from that which inspired you to buy this book in the first place.

Continue your side arc. Press your left hip out to the left slightly. Arc your torso over to your right. As you arc, feel your right ear dropping down toward your right shoulder. Relax your neck. Breathe. Come back to center and do the same on the other side. Press the right hip out to the right and arc your torso over to your left.

After you've done this a couple of times, add an arm stretch. Lift up your left arm, reaching with the fingers toward the ceiling of your bathroom. Feel the ribs on your left side lengthening. Imagine yourself getting more space *between* each rib. Do you think of your ribs as part of a fixed, unmovable cage? Not so, you have muscles between the ribs that permit the rib cage to expand and contract as you breathe. Visualize those muscles opening and stretching.

Keeping a sense of length on the left side, arc again to the right. This time let your right arm slide down the outside of your right leg. Allow the stretch to happen without tightening in your shoulder or neck. If your neck starts feeling tight, gently and slowly move it around. Relax the jaw and facial muscles. Breathe. Come back to center position.

Repeat on the other side. Do it several times on each side. Remember! Slow as the proverbial molasses.

Next let's warm up your knees by doing a few knee bends. Still standing with your feet about hip width apart and toes pointing forward, slowly bend and straighten your knees. Let the knee bends be subtle. You're not plunging down into the stance of a Red Sox catcher. You're not doing a deep knee bend à la Baryshnikov. Easy does it! Here's a way to measure how far to come into your knee bend: Imagine your back is up against a wall and you're slowly sliding down it. At most come down the imaginary wall five or six inches.

Take a moment to look down. Check to see if your knees are going directly over the toes. Your knees aren't going over your toes today? No sweat. (Everybody's anatomy is different!) Gently work toward this goal.

Next lift your head. Continue to bend and straighten the knees very slowly. Elongate the spine. Feel the neck as a continuation of the back, neither drooping forward nor held rigidly back. Relax the shoulders. Breathe. Do five or six times. If you have any discomfort or pain in your knees, stop doing this exercise at once and move on to the next one.

Now let's go for some hip circles. Keeping your knees slightly bent, bring your hips over to your right, back, to your left, and forward. Do you remember the hula hoop craze? The motion is exactly the same. Let your hips gyrate. Cut loose. Nobody's around to stare. After a few circles, reverse and go in the opposite direction. Be sure to keep your knees bent *throughout* the hip circle!

Your morning shower stretch is complete. Today as you walk toward your car, bus, or train, notice how your spine feels. Notice how *you* feel. You may detect a little extra bounce in your step. You may find yourself feeling unaccountably upbeat. You might even find yourself slightly addicted, with a yen to stretch your back at odd moments *throughout* the day.

You've come to the right place. Keep on reading.

esc

# If You're Already Zooming: Slowing Down

This morning make an intention to *notice* the speed with which you dash through your morning tasks. The way you "jump into the shower" says it all. You may not be participating in the Olympic long jump but already you're at full tilt. See if you can observe yourself with an objective eye, almost as if you were viewing one of those TV shows where a camera is parked in every room—and the subject is yourself.

Do you lather up at a breakneck speed? Do you sprint from the bathroom to the bedroom? Yank your shirt off the hanger? (If you're positively sluggish in the morning, turn to another chapter, perhaps "In the Shower.") Keep noticing. What about the way you jam papers into your briefcase? Gulp coffee?

I'll bet my pajamas you could perform each one of these acts more slowly. And do so without losing time. In fact, you may even *save* time. (Later in this chapter you'll discover why.) How about adopting a more moderate pace?

Try moving like a tectonic plate. You may ask, "Tectonic what?" Humor me for a moment—this is a beguiling way to slow down. Take two minutes. Sit down in a chair, come into the Egyptian Pose, and start some long, deep breaths. As you may have learned in geology umpteen years ago, the earth's crust is constantly being destroyed and renewed. There's a series of panels, called tectonic plates, that float along on top of molten material. The plates meet at seams, somewhat like the stitching on a tennis ball. Molten material wells up at the seams. Sometimes the plates push away from one another. Other times they collide.

As a result of this activity, the position of the continents is shifting, exquisitely slowly. (Eons from now a map of our planet will be radically different.) The Atlantic Ocean is widening, the Pacific Ocean is narrowing, and North America is edging in a westerly direction. Keep breathing. Long, deep breaths.

Beneath your feet at this very moment these wondrous geologic forces are at work. Scientists have measured the sedate, steady pace. The Atlantic Ocean, for example, is widening at the rate of three-quarters of an inch each year.

Already impatient? Mumbling to yourself, "I don't have time for a geology lesson. I've got to get going!" Take a couple more breaths, and stick with this exercise. It's going to make you feel calmer and more centered as you begin your day.

Now get out of your chair and walk at a moderate pace to your next task. Walking into the bedroom? Halfway there, stop. Breathe. Think of the mysterious forces at work beneath your feet. The slow, steady rhythm of the planet transforming itself.

Heading into the kitchen? After a few steps, stop. Just for a second. Take a couple more breaths. Think tectonically. Of course a tectonic plate doesn't think. But if it did? It would take the long view. Put things in the perspective of geologic time. A minute is inconsequential. A day the merest speck of time. A millennium's still a trifle. A million years? Now you're talking. Yes, 200 million years ago all of the continents were joined together in one giant land mass. In another 100 million years . . .

Conduct a mini-experiment. Select an activity you normally race through. Let's say you're addicted to fast showers. Slow it down. Your shower will not be a luxurious lather suited to an expensive spa. However, try washing more consciously. Instead of hastily scrubbing the same limb four times, you might only do it *once*! No need to scour as if you were caught in a sandstorm in the Sahara last night.

Moving at a more moderate pace, you'll find you actually save time because you don't have so many minor mishaps along the way. Lathering more slowly, you might find you drop the soap less often. Neither do you knock over the shampoo bottle. I'm not saying you're a klutz, but being in a hurry has this unfortunate downside. Mini-accidents happen pretty routinely—so routinely that you probably don't even notice them. Yet they have an impact on how you feel as you begin your day.

Those little mishaps are frustrating. They make you *feel* more harried. They also make you feel stupid. (Not a good way to begin the day.) Sometimes the hastily completed motion results in a problem that, in fact, does rob you of time, as when you accidentally leave the shower stall door open. Water sprays all over the floor and you have to take those precious extra minutes to mop it up.

Keep breathing. Select another morning activity to do more deliberately; for example, grabbing a coffee cup out of the dishwasher and splashing coffee into it. Do it a *tad* more slowly, breathing all the while. Notice how it feels to put your hands on the cup. Become aware of the sensation in your shoulder and neck as you lift the mug out of the drainer. Gently place the cup down on the counter. Pour the coffee unhurriedly. Imitate the pace of a fastidious waiter at a fancy restaurant who is supremely careful not to spill one drop on the white tablecloth.

Keep reminding yourself of that imperturbable, yet determined tectonic plate inching along. Sedately. Calmly. Keep breathing. Relish the feeling of being less rushed.

esc

# Before You Walk Out the Front Door: Three-Minute Mental Focusing

Sit down in a quiet place. Come into the Egyptian Pose and take some long, deep breaths. Review some of the illusions with which you begin your day. Question: How much control do you have over your commute? *Honest* answer: Not much. The unexpected is veering your way. A swarm of rubberneckers gaping at an accident. Two thousand pink grapefruits careening onto the highway from a jackknifed tractor-trailer. Icicles on the railroad tracks.

All of us know "stuff happens." Where you get in trouble is thinking you can control or change these external events. Those comforting messages flood your brain: "I'll take a side road. I'll switch into a faster lane. I'll talk to the station manager." Yet usually these remedies are ineffective. You can't change what happens around you.

Right now, make an intention to breathe when the first untoward event occurs. At first blush, making an *intention* to breathe may seem silly—or downright insulting. Here you are a high-powered professional and we're telling you to do something you do all the time. Why do you need to plan this? Because you've been breathing a totally different way for most of your life. You've a habitual way of doing everything from brushing your teeth (back molars first) to dunking a tea bag (two dunks). No surprise that you also have a breathing habit.

To shift that habit is going to take a bit of focus. Relax, you're not going to change each one of the approximately 25,000 breaths you take each day. You're going to add a new talent to your already vast repertoire: breathing differently—from time to time—during your commute.

What's nifty about changing your breathing is that it's effortless. But you do need a plan. Let's return to the concept of intention. What you plan has a chance of happening. Thinking of moving to Colorado? Really want to live in a clean city next to those gorgeous Rocky Mountains? Then you'll set in train a sequence of actions that will make the move happen. Look for a job in Denver, put your place up for sale, hire movers, find a school for Junior.

To change your breathing habits also requires a bit of planning. Here are three simple steps:

One, practice diaphragmatic breathing as described in "Are You Breathing?"

Two, plan to wear clothing that will allow you to breathe more freely. No, you don't have to buy a new wardrobe. But do remember to loosen tight belts and waistbands for the duration of your commute. Don't worry—nobody on the highway or train will notice.

Three, select a couple of breathing cues for your commute. These will be sights or sounds that will be reminders for you to breathe deeply. For example, the honk of a horn, the sound of an ambulance siren, a red light. Make your cue a simple, obvious one. Which cue you select depends upon your environment. You're briskly speeding along a crowded highway? Brake lights might be an excellent choice. Driving in the city? A red traffic light might be a handy cue. Be sure your cue occurs neither too frequently nor too infrequently. A redhead in a convertible is a poor cue. (Too rare!) A gray car is also a bad choice. (Too common.)

What's dandy about this little game: Your cue arrives at the precise moment when you're likely to get hot under the collar. Up ahead you see a horde of cars grinding to a halt. Instead of thinking, "Blast, another tie-up," your message to yourself is, "Oh yeah, time to breathe."

Be patient with yourself if you find yourself forgetting your cues. You're building a new habit. If you were learning Swahili, it would take a little time. So does learning to breathe differently. As you practice this, you'll notice those unpleasant physical symptoms of an upset—tight gut, clenched jaw, a headache—melting away.

So the next time someone's leaning on his horn, smile. It's just your cue.

# Commuter Special: By Car and by Train

# Four Years Behind the Wheel: Physical and Mental Comforts

One hour *per* day. This is the amount of time you'll spend in your car, says the U.S. Department of Transportation, if you're the average American commuter. It adds up to sixteen days behind the wheel each and every year. Hey, that's the length of your annual vacation.

Hold on to your seat belt. The figure's going to zoom higher. The average American drives from a sweet sixteen to, at least, sixty-five. That's forty-nine years. Forty-nine *x* sixteen days = two *years* spent in the driver's seat. Heck, you could earn an MBA in that amount of time. (These figures are for women. Men log in even more time.)

Live in a major urban area like Los Angeles? One hour per day may seem like an absurdly low figure. Let's say your average commute is two hours per day. Add a modest three additional hours per week of zipping down to the mall or hauling kids to baseball practice and ballet lessons. Factor in driving up to a rented cabin in the mountains on summer weekends, plus a couple of vacations at Yosemite or Glacier National Park. By the time you're sixty-five, your total may have topped *four* years behind the wheel. Long enough to have finished medical school! And who says you're going to stop driving at sixty-five?

Remember how frequently you complain about not having enough time? Practice seeing your commute as a gift of time *between* here and there. Before you say, "Bah, humbug!," humor me for a moment. What you *are* doing isn't working, so why not give a different approach a whirl? Let go of the concept that there are obstacles, hurdles, obstructions between you and your destination. Your commute *is* your destination. It's an opportunity.

You protest, "I hate this commute." Face it, steadfastly hanging on to the belief that you have to despise your commute is going to make it very hard to transform the experience. Anticipate hating, you'll get hating. You can make a choice here. You could dedicate your commuting stint to an activity you've been dying to do for ages.

First of all make a decision to get comfortable. Your back has a natural curve in the lower back, or lumbar spine. This is the area at the back of your waist. Most car seats give inadequate support to this area. Bucket seats look snappy in the ads, but they're too soft to provide firm enough support for your buttocks or back. Whenever you slump down in the car seat with your butt close to the edge of the seat, your lower back will sink into a curve, compressing the lower back disks. This is a recipe for back problems.

To avoid lower back strain while driving? Sit with your buttocks up against the seat back and gently elongate the spine up toward the roof of the car. Also get an adjustable back cushion. Check out the Internet for back supports. For example, www.relaxtheback.com has an excellent selection of pillows, wedges, and lumbar supports. If you're near one of their stores (they have stores in more than thirty-six states), it's best to go in and "test-drive" the pillows.

For your mental comforts: Get to know a composer or performer. Whether that's Bach or Sweet Honey in the Rock, try on some *unfamiliar* music. Treat yourself to jazz, African drumming, bluegrass, Gregorian chants, or songs of the humpback whale. If you're expanding your musical horizons, you'll feel less trapped by the sea of stationary cars around you.

Please include in your repertoire soothing, calm sounds. (You'll need them for the inevitable bumper-to-bumper tie-up.) Check out the New Age music section of your local record store or click into one of the Web sites that specializes in relaxing music. Warning: If it's late at night and you're tired, relaxing music could be *too* soothing! Choose a more lively selection.

Tempted to rely on your local disc jockey for your musical selections? He may have great taste, but it's not yours. Respect your unique personality and make your own selections. Choosing your music will also give you a satisfying feeling of being more in control in a basically out-of-control situation.

Music is not your bag? This is a wonderful time to explore all those books you never have time to read. Take advantage of the *years and years* of being stalled in traffic that are ahead of you. From your local library, check out books on tape. Research the audiocassette section of your local bookstore. Or you might start swapping CDs with commuting friends.

Listen to an Alice Walker novel. Catch up with Garrison Keillor. Brush up your Shakespeare. Introduce yourself to authors you wouldn't normally read. You may not be able to speed down the highway, but you can fast-forward into a genre you've never explored. Maybe it's time to check out the wisdom of the Dalai Lama. Or delve into tapes on mind-body medicine, anti-aging, and spiritual healing. They're available through www.soundstrue.com.

Caution: Do *not* wear headphones while driving. You could have an accident—if you don't hear the honk of a car whose lane you're drifting into. Listening to your novel is too engrossing to drive safely? Turn it off. Ditto if the weather is bad (icy or slick roads), traffic is tricky, or you're traveling fast. Avoid any distractions; *concentrate* on your driving. At all times be sure to keep the volume low enough on your cassette player to be able to hear motorists around you. Also please seriously consider staying away from your cell phone. According to a 1997 *New England Journal of Medicine* study, cell phone users are four times more likely to have accidents than non-users.

Think up your own unique, imaginative ways to make your trip more comfortable and enjoyable.

# The Traffic Jam: Enjoy the View

You've driven this route more than a thousand times. You think you know every tree in the median, every rest area, every inch of asphalt like the back of your hand. Not so. No matter how observant you are, you routinely miss dozens of wonders along your commute.

Next time you're tied up in a traffic jam, survey your surroundings. See if you can look at your local landscape with an inquiring glance. Sure, you've driven by this white birch countless times. But there's still something you haven't seen. The way the lower branches hang a sharp left. The bird's nest tucked up against the trunk.

If you were a resident of Moscow ogling the wonders of the USA for the first time, the birch might blow you away. (I once met a Slav who'd been told that white birches, a particular favorite of Russians, grew *only* in Russia.) If you were a seventeenth-century Native American, the birch would have a different appeal. You'd avidly study the mottling on the trunk, its straightness and height. Was it suited to become a birch bark canoe?

What about the grass alongside the highway? Peppered with trash? Not worth a second glance? You're right, it's not a lush, sylvan glade. But that dusty grass has its own wonders. I remember hearing about a scientist who measured some grass roots. First, he carefully separated the roots from the ball of soil. Second, he delicately washed and divided the roots. Third, he measured them. The length of the roots when laid out end to end? Three hundred and fifteen miles! Thanks be to the curious turn of mind that makes a scientist measure improbable things.

Next time you're irked by a traffic jam, contemplate the miles of roots thrusting underground in the "boring" median by your side. Add a horde of ants and other insects crawling about in that intricate network of roots and soil, and you have a lively microcosm.

You don't have to love ants to distract yourself from the boredom and frustration of a traffic jam. The point is that all around you is a fascinating universe. Let your full stop be a time to enjoy sky, clouds, trees, grass, birds and, of course, humans.

You may be stuck on the asphalt surrounded by suburban ticky-tack. At a superficial glance the houses all look alike. But in each one of those houses is a fascinating collection of Homo sapiens. There may be a budding Horowitz or a talented neurosurgeon-to-be. It may be the home of an extremely dedicated social worker who is bringing happiness to thousands of wheelchair-bound children. Examine the houses with a new curiosity.

That man mowing the lawn. What *is* he thinking? It's probably not about the mileage of the root structure beneath his grass! The woman peeping out of a kitchen window? Is she a single working mom at home with a sick kid? Behind each window and door is a story. A story funny, weird, boring, sad, and wonderful. Each one is worth a thousand Academy Awards.

In an urban area? Gaze at the intricate tapestry of clouds and sky reflected in plate-glass windows. The shapes and colors shifting and turning are full of surprises. Observe a church steeple against the sky. The steeple appears to sway slightly, as clouds move behind it. Enjoy the shadow of a tree on a brick wall. It's amazing how pleasurable looking freshly at ordinary things can be.

Keep looking all around you, even if you have to crane your neck. Let your eye trace the designs of pediments, cornices, and gutters. Enjoy the odd little corners where an architect cut loose his fancy. Note trees and shrubs peeking over balconies. Who knows, you might even see a hawk winging by!

The traffic jam has broken up. Continue on your trip. Next time you grind to a halt, look around as if you were a poet, or a cub reporter on her first assignment. Let your eyes and imagination roam!

# The Body Scan: How to De-stress While Behind the Wheel

Driving 3,000 pounds of steel down a crowded interstate requires lots of focus. But a clenched jaw or rigid neck is not going to make you a safer driver—quite the contrary. Tensing muscles unnecessarily is fatiguing, and the more fatigued you are, the less alert you are.

Let's scan through your body, see what's uptight, and discover a relaxing remedy. You can do this series of mini-relaxations while driving down the highway and in the midst of traffic jams.

Check out your fingers. Are you gripping the steering wheel as if it's a life raft and you're afloat in a shark-infested sea? Even if the steering wheel is covered in the finest Naugahyde, your taut fingers start a chain reaction. It goes like this . . .

Many of the muscles that move the wrist and fingers zip right up the forearm and attach to the humerus, the bone above the elbow. Tense the fingers and wrist and the entire forearm becomes rigid as steel. Next time you're at a traffic light, take one hand off the steering wheel. Make a clenched fist with this hand. (As you're doing this, be sure *not* to lock eyes with anybody via your or their rearview mirror. They might misinterpret your fist and see it as a threatening gesture.)

Note how the forearm immediately contracts. You'll also feel the tenseness traveling up into your upper arm and shoulder. Your biceps contract, your shoulder stiffens. Imagine driving for forty-five minutes in this rigid state. No wonder you frequently arrive at your destination with cramped, uptight muscles and feeling like you've been through a wringer.

Now practice driving down the highway letting your hands be loose and relaxed. Please don't do this while twiddling with the radio dial, inserting a CD, or chatting on your cell phone. Keep a firm connection with the steering wheel. At the same time, be aware of your fingers. Do they seem unnecessarily rigid? Allow them to hold on with a little less pressure on the wheel. You might even lift a couple of fingers on *one* hand. Wave them around a bit. Be sure to do this with only *one* hand at a time. Imagine you're a flutist playing a Mozart trill. Breathe. Now do the other hand.

If you're the kind of racy driver who dangerously speeds down the highway, one hand wildly gesticulating and a total of two fingers of the other hand barely touching the steering wheel, do *not* do this exercise. (Also have your head examined.) This exercise is for two-handed drivers only!

As you continue your drive, periodically ask yourself, "Are my fingers relaxed?" Then let them soften and become less stiff.

Notice your wrists. Are they as stiff as the proverbial board? Next time you're stopped in traffic, lift one hand off of the steering wheel and gently make circles with the wrist. Do the circles slowly. Rotate in each direction. Keep breathing. Return this hand to the wheel before you do your other hand.

As you continue down the highway, pay attention to your shoulders. Are you hunched forward over the wheel? Are your shoulders trying to become earmuffs? Relax your shoulders. Let them drop down. Next time the traffic grinds to a halt, do a shoulder shrug. With your arms hanging loosely and slightly bent elbows, lift your shoulders up toward your ears. Hold for a few seconds then let them drop down. Do it three to five times.

What's happening with your neck? Feel like it's in a vise? The muscles taut as a prize fighter's? At the next full stop, gently and slowly move your head side to side. With an elongated spine, slowly turn to look over your right shoulder. Hold for a moment, taking in a deep breath. Release. Turn to look over your other shoulder. Breathe again.

What about your jaw? Feel as if rigor mortis is setting in? For this one you don't have to wait for a traffic jam or red light. Notice your jaw. Drop your jaw down, open super-wide, as if the doctor were about to peer down your throat with a flashlight. Close your mouth and relax. Do it a couple of times.

Try moving your jaw around. Wiggle your chin side to side. Open and shut your mouth. (Again make sure you're not looking directly at another driver as you do this. They might think you were mouthing epithets!) Make circles with the jaw, chew as if your molars were pulverizing a big chunk of gooey caramel. Be noisy. Maybe even make some AHHH sounds.

Repeat whenever you feel you're tensing up.

# Driving More Calmly: Thinking of Fellow Commuters As "We"

It's happening to you. More and more often, your temper is flaring up on the highway. And the traffic seems to be getting steadily worse. That's because it *is* worse. Just look at the math. The number of registered vehicles has doubled since 1970. Yet the total number of miles of new road has grown by just 6 percent. That's with over $98 billion per year being spent on maintaining old and constructing new highways. The battle is being lost. No matter how many miles of interstate crush forests and pave over meadows, highway construction can't keep up with all those automobiles tumbling off assembly lines.

The solution to insane traffic in Bangkok? Drive between 2 and 4 A.M.! You may not be thrilled by this middle-of-the-night option. Why not transform your increasingly agitated feelings toward all the other folk cluttering up the interstate? Practice "We."

Do this one a few times *off* of the highway. Try it on a weekend in a quiet place in your home. Imagine you're in a traffic jam. As far ahead of you as you can see, shining metal and brake lights going on and off. Cars racked up like the parking lot at the Super Bowl. A sea of stationary hunks of metal. For Pete's sake, you could walk to work on the roofs of these cars.

Just thinking about this scenario may make you get hot under the collar. Take some long, deep breaths. Now take a moment to think about the people *inside* those metal boxes. What about all those examples of living, breathing humanity? The folk who, along with you, are equally responsible for clogging up the highways.

Now imagine yourself on one of your morning commutes. What do you have in common with your fellow drivers? Focus on some of the aspects of their lives that you share. Just like you, they all just got up. Were they up in the night comforting a kid with a broken arm? Did they propose to their girlfriend at 1 A.M.? No telling what emotional roller coasters kept them up to the wee hours.

On a typical workday, your own morning can be pretty hectic. Draw on your own experience to imagine what makes your fellow drivers irritable. A faucet handle falling off in the shower? A teenager whining through breakfast?

Those folks sitting in boxes of tanklike steel are vulnerable humans. Startlingly unique individuals. If you encountered them innocently walking down the street, you'd never dream of cursing them out. Keep on breathing. It's a new skill to think about your fellow commuters with a little sympathy and concern.

Something else you all share: You're not too fond of your commute. You dislike traffic jams. You hate bad drivers. You get angry when people endanger your life. You think you're a better driver than most other people on the road. Odd, isn't it? Everybody believes the other guy is a lousy driver. Whose perception is off? Yours? Or theirs?

It could be that they, whoever they are, are *excellent* drivers. But sometimes they do something dim-witted. Ask yourself, "Have I ever done something stupid on the highway?"

Keep breathing. What would happen if you started thinking about your fellow commuters as "we"? Me and them together. We. Of course you already do this. You're a nice, thoughtful person. Your rational mind is quite happy to think about other drivers with considerable tolerance. In your gut, it's another matter. Grrrr. They get in your way. Make you late for work. Blah-blah.

Breathe. Whatever your story is, everybody else out there has his or her story. Their story is just as urgent, fascinating, compelling as yours—at least to them.

Your commuting pals are all fundamentally kind people. They worry when their spouses, children, and friends are unhappy or ill. They want the best education for their kids. They want to live a long, productive life. In short, you have oodles in common with those perfect strangers on the highway.

Sure, some folks out there you might not choose for your best friend. Others are selfish or even crooks. Some *are* terrible drivers. Most are just plain folk. Going to work, going home. Going to work, going home. Just like you, prone to an occasional error of judgment.

As you sit comfortably in your home, make a commitment regarding your next commute. Decide to let go of behavior that will separate and divide you from the "we" of your fellow travelers. Dispense with switching from lane to lane. Forget glaring in the rearview mirror. Give up mouthing or muttering insults. And keep a safe, comfortable distance from the car in front of you.

After you've practiced thinking about your commuters in a new way while sitting in your home, take your skills out onto the freeway. The first few times you sally forth, expect to get irritated. You've been grumbling at the drivers of automobiles around you for years, and your feelings won't change immediately. If you get angry, notice your anger. "Oh, there I go, getting angry." Then let your upset drift off into the cosmos.

Patiently refocus on the people *inside* the cars. Living, breathing fathers, mothers, daughters, sons, lovers, friends to somebody. Everybody connected in a web of relationships. Folk sharing your humanity. We. Traveling together down the same highway, the same river of life.

# Driving More Calmly, Take Two:
## Being Kinder—To Your Heart

You've heard the term "road rage," but doubtless you don't think of yourself as a road rager. There's a big difference between someone bashing in another person's car trunk with a golf club and you. You're a smart, competent person efficiently driving your two teenage sons to soccer practice.

Yet you'll admit you do have *those* moments. Moments when you've felt a surge of animosity when somebody cuts in front of you. Times when you want to scream at the driver behind you; he's been tailgating you for miles! You often arrive at your destination tired, angry and with a pounding headache. Stressed out. Yet on some level you think it's no big deal. A part—albeit an unpleasant one—of life in the twenty-first century.

It's time to think of your health.

As we've already seen in "Quick Anatomy Lesson," in an emergency your whole physiological system gets primed to jump out of the way of an out-of-control car or an oncoming bus, or to run from a fire. Even if the emergency is not actual, but perceived ("I hate that guy"), your respiratory rate increases, blood pressure goes up, your heartbeat becomes more rapid, and a host of other complex systems in your body are activated.

At the same time, your body starts to release stress hormones, such as adrenaline and steroids. These nifty chemicals allow your body to sustain its emergency response system. What's not so nifty is that these hormones *hang around* long after the stressful event has ended. For example, the guy you were so angry at has pulled off the highway. He got lost, but the stress chemicals are not so easily discouraged. Some of them will stay in your bloodstream for hours. They keep you *feeling* hyped up. Stress hormones also help to keep your blood pressure up. Add a little chronic anger and irritation (which is *also* elevating your blood pressure) to the mix, and you have a problem.

In a sense your whole system is revving up. Keep revving and it will have an impact on your health. Studies now clearly link chronic stress with a weakened immune system. At exam time, students do get more colds! There's also a correlation between chronic stress, hypertension (high blood pressure), and the health of your heart.

You may be too young to be worrying about your heart, but it's likely you're already thinking about your financial future. How about viewing your health in the same way? Why not acquire some stress-reduction habits that will decrease your susceptibility to problems later? Put some calmness into your savings account. So here are some tips to make your drive more serene and less stressful.

Put on some soothing music.

Take a deep breath *every time* somebody cuts in front of you or does something else stupid. Take a deep breath *every time* the traffic slows. Take a deep breath *whenever* you find yourself muttering and cursing, "That jerk!" "That blankety-blank!" Take a deep breath *every time* you notice you're late. As you're breathing, give yourself a gentle little self-talk. "Oh, there I go growling again." Make light of whatever is going on. "Silly me."

Take a deep breath and look at the photos on your dashboard. What photos, you ask?

You probably don't have a photo on your dashboard. Not yet. Consider getting one. You have a picture of your honey, your wife and kids, your poodle in your wallet and on your desk at work. What pleasure it gives you to lift your eyes from the tedium of a spreadsheet and gaze at a photo of your two-year-old grinning to beat the band. It was taken on a wonderful hike in the Adirondacks last summer. One look at that photo and you can practically smell the fresh blueberries you picked!

Why not give yourself the possibility of the same lift in your auto? Try using one of those plastic photo holders with a magnet. Put your memento of a close friend, a sibling, or your family on the dashboard. The next time you're about to lock eyes with a "bad" driver, immediately switch your gaze over to the photograph. Take some long, deep breaths. Call to mind a special moment with the person in the photo. Breathe some more.

Next time the traffic grinds to a halt? Look at your sweetie. Breathe. Believe me, just looking at the photo and breathing *shallowly* isn't going to make much difference. You need to really *practice* your deep, diaphragmatic breathing skills here.

As the weeks go by, from time to time, change the photo. What about that amazing shot of your best friend hiking in the High Sierras? The inspiring view of migrating whales off of Point Reyes? The ocean at sunset? Whatever images thrill you, take with you.

Combine these tips with the practice of seeing other commuters as "we," and you'll arrive at your destination calmer, less agitated. Perhaps—surprise, surprise—even happy!

Want more information on the biology of the stress response? Check out *Why Zebras Don't Get Ulcers: An Updated Guide to Stress, Stress-Related Diseases, and Coping*, by Robert Sapolsky.

esc

# Good Morning: Two Magic Words

Do you zip off to work like one of those old-fashioned (circa 1930) department store pneumatic tubes? You step into a tube—your commuter train, for example—surround yourself with a cocoon of hostile, keep-your-distance vibes, and silently ricochet off to your destination?

There's another way. Planet Earth's inhabitants have been saying "Good Morning" for centuries. Even in Shakespeare's time, folks were strutting about in their codpieces saying it. All over the world, people keep saying it. Just as you're tucking your six-year-old into bed, someone in Japan is rolling off his tongue, *Ohayō Gozaimasu*. In Europe it may be *Buenos Dias* or *Bonjour*.

Living in a crowded urban area, like Chicago or Boston? You probably reserve this friendly expression for family and friends. Maybe it's a greeting you share with your newspaper vendor or the coffee-shop man. Resident of a small town or the 'burbs? You may say it more often than your urban counterpart. Yet, I bet there's someone you see in the morning but act as if they don't exist.

There's definitely something powerful about these two words. They keep bouncing around the globe. *Buon Giorno, Dzień Dobry, Dobro Jutro*.

How about saying "Good Morning" to a person you encounter on your commute, someone you usually ignore? Pick somebody official: the ticket agent or train conductor. I suggest picking someone official so there are no misunderstandings. No unwanted come-ons. It also feels pleasant to make contact in a friendly fashion with a person who is providing *you* with a service.

Take a few deep breaths as you're standing on the train platform. Contemplate the millions of people all over the United States, as well as in different countries, who are saying their particular version of "Good Morning." It's almost like a chorus of birds chirping away. *Joreggelt Kivanok. Guten Morgen.*

Be aware of your tone of voice as you greet the conductor. If you sound gruff or hostile, she's going to believe your voice, not your words. Also notice where you're looking. Are you staring at her arm? Eyes burrowing into the collar of her shirt? Try shifting your eyes upward. Look at her face.

When you first start doing this, notice what you're feeling as you speak. See if you can say your greeting without *any* expectation regarding how they should or will respond. They don't quickly reply, "Good Morning"? Okay. Perhaps they didn't hear you. Could be the last person who spoke to them chewed them out. Now, hearing something friendly, they can't believe their ears. Frankly, it doesn't matter how they react. What matters is that you reached out to a fellow human being.

After you've said "Good Morning" for a few days in a row, escalate your friendliness. If the conductor is turned toward you, look him or her in the eyes. This one is tricky. Looking a stranger in the eyes requires sensitivity. Let your eyes be soft, friendly. Usually you'll find a slightly pleased person looking back at you. She may even be grateful.

Grateful? Yes. How would you like to be bombarded by cross and snippy comments all day? Or, perhaps worse, totally ignored? How would you like to be pacing up and down the cars punching tickets? Send a little understanding glance at your conductor. Both you and she will feel better.

One or two words of kindness and suddenly your own problems are lighter. The cares of your world are less burdensome. By the way, if you imagine you don't have to say these two words because somebody else will, think again. Next time you're on the train, sit down and observe how many passengers speak in a friendly manner to the conductor. If you're in a major metropolitan area and it's rush hour, it's may be once in a blue moon.

By the way, your greeting may set a trend. It makes it easier for the next rider to say, "Good Morning," if they have heard your words. Being upbeat before 8 A.M. just too much for you today? Can't force "Good Morning" from between your lips? Here's an alternative: Sit down and observe the other passengers getting onto the train. Imagine saying "Good Morning" to the next three people who get on. Look at them and silently think the words as they clamber aboard. It doesn't matter whether you like the shape of their eyebrows, the expression on their faces, or the newspaper they're carrying. Internally say "Good Morning" to them. Even though your words are inaudible, just thinking them will make you feel a bit more agreeable, less on edge.

Once you become proficient with "Good Morning," you'll want to add some phrases to the lexicon of what you say out loud. "Thank you," "Have a nice day," "Enjoy the holiday." Sounds corny? Maybe it is. But you and a stranger will begin the new day with a lift, a spark, a zest.

Try out your random friendliness with toll collectors, bus drivers, a subway conductor. If you are already saying it to these folks, pick someone else. A sanitation man is one of my favorites. Garbage collectors are often shunned. One "Good Morning" and they (and you) will be really surprised!

*esc*

# Coping with Crowds: Letting Go of "Faster Is Better"

You're at a train station amidst a horde of humanity. It's moving at the pace of a severely handicapped clam. Eight people abreast are being funneled into one up escalator. So what can you do?

First—you've got it—breathe. Wherever you are, stand still for a moment and breathe. Long, deep breaths.

Second, become aware of your spine. Gently elongate the spine and lengthen the back muscles. Do this without shrugging or hunching your shoulders. Feel your feet pressing into the floor. Press down equally with each foot. Breathe some more—nice diaphragmatic breathing.

Next, remind yourself that there's absolutely nothing you can do to change the *external* circumstance of your current situation. (Unless you decide to turn back and go wherever you're going on another day. Or decide you'll never go to this particular place.) Cast a cold, clear eye at the physical limits of your situation. Doesn't it boil down to a simple shuffle? You can edge forward, putting one foot in front of another. Left foot. Right foot. Right foot. Left foot.

What if you gave up the need to get there, wherever "there" is, faster? What if you abandoned the idea—just for the next ten minutes—that it was desirable to increase your forward motion? You'd suddenly be free. Free to explore the mental possibilities of your situation.

Free? Isn't that a stupidly loaded word to use for the situation of being packed in like the proverbial sardines? Hmmm. Keep breathing. Yes, nagging thoughts will flood your brain. "Why don't they schedule more trains?" "Why didn't I leave home earlier?" Notice the thoughts. Let them float by.

Give up the notion that you need to get to the escalator faster, and you can forego competing with your fellow crowd members. You may laugh outright at this suggestion. You've been competitive since you were two and your sister stole your dump truck. Competition got you a scholarship to college. It's propelling you to the top of your law firm.

Face it. Dog-eat-dog doesn't work in this crowd. See what happens when you stop competing. Yes, generally keep your place. But when a pushy fellow shoulders his way ahead of you, let him pass. He thinks he's got to get there thirty seconds ahead of you? That's his problem. Let him "win." Keep on breathing. Ditto with the woman you noticed behind you a few moments ago. She has now edged her way in front of you. Let her "win."

I'm not suggesting being a doormat. If somebody steps on your toe or elbows you in the ribs, resolutely protest. Forget, however, about evening a score. Just keep breathing.

Dr. John Larson, author of *Road Rage to Road-Wise*, an excellent book on managing temper tantrums on the highway, has useful advice. On a crowded highway, silently greet each driver who cuts in front of you with, "Be my guest." I'm not saying you're in the midst of a temper tantrum. Yet you *do* feel on the brink.

Next time someone jostles in front of you think, "Be my guest." "Age before beauty . . ." "After you . . ." Drag the old chestnuts out. Mentally saying these words will make you feel slightly more friendly to the type-A personality who's nipping at your heels.

So he's passing you. Beating you. Big deal. You might even consider sending him or her a drop or two of compassion. That rude behavior suggests a stress-and-heart-disease-prone dude.

Are you breathing? Check in with your spine. Is it still elongated? Are your shoulders relaxed? Is your neck soft? Take a few more shuffling steps. Let the breath deepen. Full, long breaths.

Ceasing to compete with your fellow members of the crowd will make you feel better. Why? Because you no longer have to think ill of them. Fixated on getting to the escalator before everybody else? You'll see each of the human beings around you as an abstract concept: a competitor. And, automatically, you view your competitors in an unfavorable light. They *deserve* to be pushed aside by you. They're in some way less important, inferior, different from you. They're ugly, old, fat, not nice, pushy, aggressive. They speak a language you don't understand. You don't like the color of their hair.

These thoughts may be unconscious or conscious. But you have to *not* like the beings around you to push ahead of them. Yet it's unpleasant to dislike people, particularly ones you don't know. (At least with the folks with whom you're acquainted, you may have a valid reason!)

After all, how can you dislike people you know zilch about? That guy accidentally jabbing you in the ribs could be a real sweetie. He's adopted three foster kids. The woman right in front of you? She has kayaked across the Bering Strait three times. The man over to your right is a world-famous basketball player. Next to him is a window washer who regularly balances on narrow ledges—twenty-seven stories high. Behind you is an expert on DNA. If you were to talk to anybody in this crowd, you'd find all kinds of reasons why *they* should go first, and you should lag behind.

Breathe. Keep on shuffling. One foot in front of the next.

After several sessions of "Coping with Crowds," you'll notice a subtle change in your interior landscape. You may start to feel bizarrely fond of your next crowd. Or you may see this polyglot group of strangers as a pleasantly neutral phenomenon. You coexist with them briefly. But you'll never see them again.

# Mountain Pose:
# Stretching the Spine Inconspicuously

When it's standing room only on the train, what do you do? Sumo wrestle with the *New York Times*? Grind your teeth and groan? How about something completely different? Let's go for a gentle stretch called the Mountain Pose.

Find a pole or a handle on a seat near you with which to stabilize yourself as the train lurches, speeds up, or stops. Place one hand on the pole, letting the other arm hang down by your side. Carrying a briefcase? Put it on the floor between your feet with both of your feet touching the case, so you are aware at all times of where your briefcase is. If you have a pocketbook, sling it from the arm that is lifted.

Breathe. Long, steady breaths. Keep the knees slightly bent. This will help to stabilize you if the train suddenly stops. Press down with your feet. Feel your feet firm against the floor. Notice if you're pressing down equally with each foot. Often we favor one foot over the other. Balance the weight equally between both feet.

Start gently elongating up through the spine. Please remember I use the term "elongate" to encourage you to lift *without* stiffening or going rigid. Let the spine stretch deliciously upward. Allow a sense of fluidity and ease in the back.

Find a vertical line with which to align your back, maybe the side of a door, a frame on a window, another pole. Using that line as a guide to keep lengthening upward. Notice the shoulders. If they start hiking up toward your ears, let them drop back down. Feel the shoulder blades melting down your back.

Lift the neck gently. Feel this lengthening start in the upper back and continue up into the neck. Let the neck be relaxed. Lift up softly on either side of the neck. Imagine the neck floating on top of the spine. Are you still breathing? (Often when we concentrate we hold our breath.) Breathe long, deep breaths.

Relax your eyes. Keep them open but with a gentle, unfocused gaze. Release the jaw. Soften the facial muscles. Keep breathing.

What's happening with the arm you're using to stabilize yourself? Is it tight? Let it relax. Check out the other arm. Let it hang loosely by your side. Notice the fingers on each hand. If they're clenched, unclench them. Breathe some more.

Now bring your attention to your feet again. Feel your feet firm and solid on the floor. Press down equally with the heels and the balls of your feet. Another commuter bumps up against you? Just keep breathing.

Start imagining yourself as a mountain. Mountains are marvelous phenomena. Think of the layers of rocks in a mountain. The outcroppings of granite. The strong boulders. Mountains persevere throughout the eons. They are undaunted by snow, sleet, drenching rain, or scorching sun. Unfazed by lightning, tornadoes, and forest fires, they simply do their mountain thing. Clouds draped around their craggy tops don't vex them. Mist, hail, blizzards are all the same to these Olympian giants. Sometimes an earthquake comes along and the mountain shrugs. Otherwise it just *is*. Solid, strong, patient. Mountains don't hurry or move. They wait. Quietly.

Feel some mountain energy starting to rise up through your body. Stay with long, deep breaths. Continue softly elongating the spine. Feel yourself gradually becoming taller. Like a mountain, you're stable and calm. Sense the steadiness deep inside you. At your core, feel silence and stillness. You could stand here, swaying gently with the motion of the train, for centuries. A child starts to fuss. Ignore him. Remain focused on your mountain energy.

Now bring a slight smile to your mouth. Lift the corners of your lips the tiniest amount. You're not going for a big, Hollywood, toothpaste-ad grin. Just a soft hint of a smile. Notice any shift in your mood. (Studies have shown that the simple, mechanical act of smiling actually makes people feel better.)

Stay standing tall until you reach your destination. If you can remain tall in this circumstance, packed in with hundreds of strangers, giddily zipping (or slowly crawling, depending upon the vagaries of track construction and mechanical failures) along—well, that's amazing! Think what might happen at your work site if you were mountainlike while talking with your supervisor.

To enhance your experience of the Mountain Pose, practice it at home. In your at-home version, lift both arms overhead. The arms can either be in a V-position with the palms facing forward or lifted alongside the ears with the palms facing in. Even though you're lifting the arms, relax your shoulders. Practice a couple of times in front of a mirror. Watch to see if the shoulders are hunching up. Then move away from the mirror and practice without looking at yourself.

Stretch from your feet up to the tips of your fingers. Feel your feet pressing down into the floor. Imagine them connecting with the earth beneath the building in which you're standing. Enjoy the mountain energy coursing through your body.

Next time you practice on a train, remember what it felt like to have both arms stretching overhead. The Mountain Pose is also great for packed subways and jammed buses.

esc

# Flexing Your Compassion Muscles: Appreciating Your Fellow Commuters

Sitting on a train? Somewhat grumpily facing the morning commute? How about practicing some compassion—for the strangers around you? Come into the Egyptian Pose and start taking long, deep breaths. After a few moments, choose a person at least ten feet away. Select a child or pre-adolescent kid (no point in making the exercise really tough by homing in on a hormone-haywire teenager). A sleeping infant is good for a beginning.

Notice the child's face, eyelashes, mouth, tiny hands, fingers, and nails; observe the blankets in which he/she is wrapped, the socks on her feet, his overalls or cap. Avoid thoughts about whether you think the baby is cute or ugly, whether she/he looks comfortable or not, whether you like the look of the person holding the baby, whether you agree with the adult's methods of caregiving.

Breathe. Relax your neck and shoulders. Quietly observe. Take in this tiny being in all her vulnerability, all his fragility. After a moment or two, turn away and look at an unoccupied seat or a blank area of metal. (If you stare too long, the child's parent or caregiver may get nervous.)

Contemplate this baby's future. What opportunities will come her way? Will she finish high school? Go to college? Graduate first in her class at law school? Will she break through the glass ceiling at IBM and become a CEO? Will he become a catcher for the Mets? A conductor on the subway? A dental hygienist? The computer whiz of the century? The proud father of twins?

Look again at her tiny hands. Enjoy the miracle of her diminutive fingers. How will this baby use its fingers? Will she learn to play the piano? Will he become a master at chess? Will she become a botanist, delicately pressing seeds into experimental soils in a science laboratory? Regard the plump legs. Where will they carry this human being? Will he become a professional dancer in Broadway musicals? Will she become a firefighter scaling ladders, rescuing kids from the fierce blazes? Study the head. What thoughts will course through this brain? Will she ponder the significance of distant planets, discover new comets, offer a new theory of black holes? Will he be a brilliant strategist on a basketball court or become adept at calculus?

The possibilities are myriad. You'll never know what became of this bundle of potential sitting before you. Allow yourself to feel compassion for whatever future shock and schlock are coming this baby's way. Appreciate and feel sympathy for all the hard work, happiness, achievements, joys, loves, losses, disappointments, pain, and suffering of this vulnerable mortal.

Are you breathing? If not, please do so, as you open your heart to this particular, unique, amazing human being.

Ready to graduate from experiencing compassion for an infant to an adult? *Much harder!* Again, start with someone who's at least ten feet away. Even though you're sitting at some distance from this individual, do this calming technique discreetly, without staring. You do not want the person to feel embarrassed or uncomfortable. Nor do you want to provoke a hostile reaction. You need only look at the person a couple of times.

When selecting the adult you're going to focus on pick someone who does not press your buttons. If you see someone with a trait that you personally can't stand—nails too short or too long, oily skin, a nose ring—select another candidate. No matter whom you select, your fertile, creative mind will start judging. It's a game our minds constantly play. It's a perfectly natural defense mechanism; a way to set up a wall between ourselves and this mass of strangers with whom our destiny is temporarily linked. When you discover these critical thoughts coursing through your mind, just observe those thoughts. Sometimes it helps to label the thought, "Oh, another critical thought."

Don't hold on to the thought or follow it. Just notice it, somewhat like observing a flock of sparrows rising above a tree. You can't stop them. You let the birds pass out of your line of vision and don't worry about what happens to them next. Let your thoughts also pass on. It's almost as if you were releasing them to the universe. Breathe.

Be curious about this human being. He/she made it this far all in one piece. What kind of job does she have? She may be returning home after a day of emptying bed pans at a city hospital or defending Texaco in court. How's his personal life? Is he married happily or unhappily? Did his only daughter die in a drowning accident last year? Is she totally thrilled that, after six years of every fertility trick in the medical lexicon, she is, at long last, pregnant? What about his health? Does he have chronic back pain?

The person you have chosen to think about is a mystery. Contemplate their accomplishments, their sorrows, their secret passions. Let yourself feel sympathy for whoever they are. Allow yourself a sense of wonder. They have made it this far in their complicated and demanding lives. What an achievement! What bravery and courage!

Congratulate yourself on practicing compassion on the train. Take in a few more deep breaths. Notice how you feel after doing this exercise, both physically and mentally.

esc

# Nine to Five
# (Including
# Lunch)

# Caffeine Substitute:
# Easy Perk-up Tips

*Caffeine substitute?* Relax. I'm not going to suggest you give up coffee. The stuff tastes too darn good. From time to time, however, you might try a different stimulant. Like stretching.

Been at your computer for more than one hour? Then it's time for some action. If the mood in your office is conducive, walk around. Get your blood moving. You may ask, doesn't it move all the time? Yes, it does. But moving and stretching, plus breathing, improve your circulation. (You've already noticed this when riding on an airplane for hours at a stretch. Fluids often pool in your ankles and feet, causing painful swelling.)

So stride off to the water cooler. Step down the hall and exchange a few words with the receptionist. Walk *briskly* to the restroom. On your way there, add a quick detour: If you can get access to the stairwell, go for a bracing hike. Go down or up two flights of stairs—still maintaining a lively pace—then return to your floor.

As you walk (or climb stairs), lengthen the spine, relax the shoulders, breathe. Let your hips be open. See if you can move without tightening your buttocks or stomach. Swing your legs easily, in a relaxed fashion. Particularly be aware of your arms. If you've been at your computer, the muscles may be tight. Let your arms hang loosely by your sides. Relax the wrists, fingers, and hands. Keep breathing.

Feel chained to your desk? Can't leave? At least stand up. Stretch your arms overhead. Reach first with one arm a little bit higher, as if you were reaching up to pluck grapes off of a vine on the ceiling. Feel the ribs on that side of the torso lengthening. Then reach up with the other arm. Feel the ribs stretching on this side. If you are wearing a tight belt, loosen it before doing this stretch. Now reach up with both arms. Stretch the whole body from your feet up to the tips of your fingers. Feel the belly stretching, the back, the whole torso expanding and lengthening upward. Let the stretch be delicious.

Now give your amazing brain a boost. Your brain is one of nature's top inventions. One hundred billion cells tick away, processing millions of bits of information pouring in via your five senses. Whether you're remembering something your mom said when you were seven or calculating how many gallons of orange it takes to paint the Golden Gate Bridge, your gray matter is hopping with activity. Neurons are zipping off messages, neurotransmitters are jumping across synapses.

All this activity requires oxygen, and lots of it. The brain occupies about 5 percent of the body's weight but requires 20 percent of the body's oxygen. Unfortunately, your lifestyle often robs those precious brain cells of this wonderful fuel. You may live in a polluted urban environment, your commute may involve long traffic jams (more polluted air), and it's likely you breathe shallowly.

No surprise you feel weary before the day is half over! For this next stretch, there's a medical advisory. If you have high blood pressure and are not on medication, do *not* do this exercise. I seldom get dogmatic in *Serenity to Go,* but if you have *untreated* high blood pressure, go to your doctor to develop a treatment plan. You have diabetes? Also do not do this exercise. Folks with treated high blood pressure? It's fine to do everything in this chapter.

This is one you can do either seated in your chair or standing. If you're doing the chair version, be sure your chair is stable before starting. Your chair is on rollers? Roll it back to a place where the chair back is in contact with a solid surface like a desk or file cabinet. Now gently lean forward and come to sit with your torso resting on your thighs and your arms hanging down parallel to your feet. Let your head hang down. Start long deep breaths.

Let all your back muscles relax. Soften the shoulders and back of the neck. With each exhalation, feel your back releasing tension. Let the weight of your head pull you down a tiny bit further. Notice what's happening to the muscles around your mouth and eyes. Let them relax. Unclench your jaw. Stay here for three to five long, deep breaths.

The beauty of this pose is that helps the blood come into your brain. (This is why if you feel faint after being jabbed in the arm too many times, a doctor or nurse will ask you to lean forward.) And, as you now know, more blood means more oxygen. More blood to the head also means more glucose traveling to your brain cells. More oxygen and more glucose result in a refreshed, efficient brain. A creative, problem-solving brain.

Another advantage to this pose is that it will give you a fresh perspective on life, on your job, your supervisor, the task at hand. Seeing things upside down can be quite thrilling. Suddenly an old problem has a new solution. All at once a coworker is less irritating, a task less onerous.

Have a private office? Your office mates are out to lunch or you have access to a library or conference room where you will not feel conspicuous? Try a standing version of the upside-down pose. Stand with your buttocks against a wall and your feet about two feet apart. Bend your knees, then gradually curl your torso forward. Start with your head. Let the chin come down to the chest, let the shoulders curve forward, then bend at the waist.

This pose is not about getting somewhere. Please do *not* try to touch your toes. Just hang forward, relaxing. Let gravity gently draw your torso toward the floor. Take long, deep breaths. Relax the shoulders and arms. Allow the arms to sway a bit. Be sure to keep your eyes open. Bring a soft gaze to your eyes. (If you close your eyes, you might get dizzy.) Keep breathing.

Remember to *enjoy* your upside-down view of the world. Stay in this position for three to five long, steady breaths. Be sure to come out of this one slowly. Return to your computer refreshed and calm.

# On Hold: A Simple Face Massage

You feel like you've been on hold for a century. The canned music is driving you nuts. You're starting to think that the perky voice saying, "Your call is important to us" is a pathological liar. Instead of grinding down your back molars, how about an exquisitely easy and relaxing face massage? It's discreet, so your office colleagues will probably not notice. If they do, they may ask for pointers on how they can do it too.

To begin, notice how you're holding the phone. Are you balancing it between a hunched-up shoulder and a twisted neck? If so, please straighten your neck and move the receiver a few inches away from your ear. Don't worry, you'll still hear the party when she or he returns. Shift the phone into your nondominant hand. This sequence is designed for people who are right-handed. Sart with the phone in the left hand, leaving the right hand free to do the first half of your face massage. If you are a lefty, do the reverse.

Now make some adjustments so you can hold the phone more loosely. You're not a rock climber tied into a belaying pin on El Capitan, so there's no need to clutch the receiver as if your life depended upon it. Practice letting your fingers relax. Lightly curl and uncurl the fingers on the edge of the receiver and let the little finger wave in the air. Soften the wrist. Rotate the wrist gently from side to side. Take long, deep breaths as you're making these adjustments.

As we've seen in the "Body Scan," the muscles that control flexing and extending the wrist go right up the forearm and attach to the humerus, the bone in your upper arm. Your fingers and wrist are cramping down for dear life?

Then your whole arm, shoulder, and neck will be tight as the proverbial drum. To make holding the phone even easier, you might rest the left elbow on your desk, keeping the forearm vertical so the phone is only a few inches away from your ear. Or, to provide additional support for the phone's weight, tuck your left elbow up against your torso.

Check your spine. Keep it nice and elongated throughout this exercise. Next, imagine that your face is divided down the middle into two halves. Begin massaging the right side with your right hand. Start with the second and third fingers drawn together and gently extended. Using the pads on the tips of these fingers, start massaging your forehead. Place the fingertips between the eyebrows and press down gently. Then move the fingers out toward the hairline in a single, slow motion. Once you reach the hairline, lift the fingers off the skin and bring them back to the area between the eyebrows. Again, press down and gently smooth the skin outward. Do this several times.

Check to see that you're breathing nice, long, slow breaths. Observe what's happening with your shoulders, arms, and neck. Let them relax. Notice the facial muscles in other parts of your face, particularly around the eyes and mouth. Relax these muscles also.

Continue your massage. As you move the fingers out toward the hairline, imagine you are smoothing out any worry marks on your forehead. Your forehead is becoming smooth, as placid as a clear mountain lake on a calm day. Next move down to your right temple, the place between the edge of your eyes and the hairline in front of the ear. Start doing little circular motions with your hand and fingers. Don't lift the fingers off of the skin; let the motion of the hand create this gentle massage.

Come down into the area of the cheeks. Continue placing two or three fingers on the skin and making diminutive circular motions with the hands. Then pick up the fingers and move to another spot. Find the places in your face that are particularly tense. Experiment with doing this massage in different areas. How about close to the nose, on the outside of the cheekbone, or maybe near the corner of the mouth?

Take a moment to check in with what's happening with your left elbow. Move this elbow around gently to be sure it is not tense or locked in place. What about your left hand? Is it clenching the phone again? Soften and relax the fingers.

Now focus on your jaw muscle. It's one of the strongest muscles in the body—it has to be in order to chomp through T-bone steaks, raw carrots, and corn on the cob. It's also a lightning rod for tension. Help it to relax by doing a massage along the jaw line. Start just below the ear. Go down along the jawline doing a circular massage in several locations. Let the mouth be slightly open as you do these mini-massages. The chin should be so relaxed that it moves slightly.

If your phone call comes through and you've not yet finished your massage, you may actually be disappointed that you're no longer on hold! Finish your face massage either at the end of your phone call or when you're *next* on hold. To finish the massage, go to the other side of your face. To do this, you will need to switch the phone over to the other hand.

As you massage the other side of your face, get a little more adventuresome. Experiment with different strokes. Maybe do some gentle tapping motions, or try using the palm of your hand to massage your cheek. Perhaps focus more on the jaw, less on the forehead. Or vice versa. Find the massage your face craves.

Keep breathing. Luxuriate in your little break.

# Dance of the Eyeballs:
# An Antidote to Eyestrain

Whether you're shackled to a computer all day or copyediting a textbook, any close, detailed work is hard on the eyes. In cavewoman days, eyeballs were critical to finding dinner. And to avoiding *being* dinner. Whether your ancestor was scanning the horizon for antelope, trying to detect a hungry leopard lurking in the bush, or gathering roots for a tasty soup, she constantly moved her eyes. From near to far, from side to side, from far to near. Lots of eye movement.

For today's typical office worker, not so. For hours at a time, your eyes are focused up close. The result? The eye muscles get rigid. Didn't know you had eye muscles? These tiny muscles don't bulge like a toned biceps, but they're absolutely vital. Without them you'd be unable to shift your gaze. Tiny muscles inside the eyeball control the lens of the eye. When these delicate muscles contract, you're able to read text inches in front of your nose (for example, the words printed on this page). Relax these same muscles and you can look at the reproduction of a Van Gogh on the wall across the room. You've also got diminutive muscles on the outside of your eyeballs. These muscles move your eyes in different directions.

Problem: After prolonged close-up focus, it's hard for these muscles to relax. Additional problem: Contract any muscle consistently, and it becomes fatigued. It's weird. If you were to canoe for eight hours straight, you'd *expect* an aching back. You'd have your favorite remedies. Maybe a combination of stretching, a hot bath, and rest. Yet you assume your eyeballs can stay glued to a computer from nine to five and not suffer any ill effects.

Luckily, there's a refreshing tonic for tired eye muscles: a discreet mini-break. Start with some long, deep breaths. Relax the jaw and neck. Now focus your eyes on a distant object. Do this with a soft, slightly blurred gaze. (Eyeglass wearers will need to experiment. Farsighted? You may want to take your eyeglasses off. Folks wearing bifocals may want to keep their spectacles on. Do whatever is *comfortable* for you.)

If there's a window nearby, look out the window. Enjoy the movement of clouds, the shape of tree trunks, the shift of leaves in a breeze, the many different colors of grass. If the view is of a parking lot or highway, so be it. Let your eyes softly flow over the shapes of cars and follow the activities of passersby. Notice a black Labrador enjoying a ride in a pickup truck. Observe how a traffic light swings in the wind. Watch a bird dart by.

Become aware of *how* you're looking at the people and objects around you. If you're naturally tense and do this exercise tensely, it won't offer any relief to your eyeballs. Observe your mood as you tell the eye muscle what to do. Are you like a military sergeant barking orders, commanding the eye to look at the clouds? All the while are you thinking, "Let's get through with this as fast as possible, so I can get back to the important stuff?"

If so, try a different tack. Let the information you give your eyes be more gentle. As you're glancing around, let your vision be less hard-edged, more peripheral. Look at the blades of grass not to detect a ladybug climbing up a stem, but to see a general pattern of light and shade. Not close enough to a window to look out? Allow your eyes to gently follow the vertical and horizontal lines of the window frames. Check out what's on the windowsill.

No windows? Survey the room. Let your eyes playfully observe any items you see. A potted plant on a coworker's desk? Allow your eyes to softly take in shapes and colors. Remember, keep your eyes slightly unfocused as you do this. Let your eyes register a sweater slung over the back of a chair. Let the shapes be nothing more than an abstract pattern. Notice folds, textures, shadows. Forget about the owner of the sweater. Put aside your opinions of that person. Just observe the yarn, the pattern, the hue. Hate the color? Can't be neutral about what you're looking at? Shift your vision to another object.

Next bring your eyes to look at your knees or at the floor by your feet. Breathe. Soften the eyes even more. Notice what's happening with your shoulders. If they've become tight, let them relax. Allow your eyes to follow the pattern of curlicues, squares, or stripes in the rug. Return to the distant object, or another distant object. It doesn't matter *what* you look at. Whatever it is, glance at it curiously, gently, and softly. Take a couple more breaths. Return the gaze to your knees. Breathe some more. Go back and forth between near and far several times. Like any exercise, the key is *moderation*. Avoid flicking your eyes back and forth so rapidly that you develop a different sort of eyestrain. Easy does it.

You regularly do close work at your office? It's highly recommended that you do this exercise frequently throughout the day, maybe once every fifteen minutes. That may sound like a lot, but it'll only take you twenty to thirty seconds. And if your eyes are relaxed, you'll work more efficiently. You'll get more done and feel less fatigued at the end of the day.

A nice gift for the eyes at the conclusion of this exercise: Take your hands and quickly rub the palms one against the other for ten to fifteen seconds. When some heat has built up, cup the hands and gently place over the eyes. Feel the heat from your warm palms soothing your eyes. The reason this works? As you know, after a day of gardening, a hot bath relaxes your back. Likewise, the heat from your palms helps your tired eye muscles to relax.

Please note: If you're a person who likes to destress after a hard day at the office by "zoning out" and watching TV, remember that staring at anything *without regularly shifting your gaze* is hard on the eyeballs! So during ad breaks, move your eyes. Look at a painting on the wall, a coffee mug sitting on a table, the way a curtain billows in the wind. And keep breathing!

esc

## Deli Dance: Being Thankful While Eating Cheek by Jowl

Your lunch date fell through. Instead of holding hands and gazing romantically at your honey, you're alone, having a tuna-on-rye at the most crowded deli in town. The decibel level approximates a NASA rocket launch. Whether you realize it or not, this is the perfect time for practicing a little gratitude. Begin by thinking of the complicated chain of events that produced this particular and, you hope, tasty sandwich. Bend your mind around this question: Who were the people key to the creation of this morsel?

Who makes it onto your list depends upon your imagination. A sample of folk the luncheon roster might include: The woman at the seed manufacturer, checking for quality. The laborer who drove the tractor. He plowed the field where the seeds were planted. He also tinkered with the Deere engine to keep it humming. The engineer who designed the irrigation system that watered the lettuce. The field hand. He bent over in the hot sun, picking the lettuce. Whoa! Bending over for hours at a stretch is tough.

Send some gratitude to each of these folk. Incredulous thoughts popping up? "Thankful? No way, not when I'm surrounded by people suffering from verbal diarrhea!" Wondering, "How can I be grateful with somebody's sports page spilling over into my soup?" Breathe. Long, deep breaths. Politely ask the guy to remove his newspaper and then let your neighbors do their thing. Return to doing your thing.

Continue with your list. The seasick bloke who stayed up until 4 A.M. in a cold, driving rain on a tossing sea to pull in that amazing fish. The truck driver. He sang an old Stevie Wonder song as he blasted his semi across the continent, rushing the lettuce to your local market. The gasoline station attendant pumping diesel fuel into the six-axle semi. The waiter in the diner where you are currently munching down said sandwich. Recently arrived from Pakistan, he says "whiskey down" with the greatest aplomb. It's astounding the web of humanity that labored hard and long to deliver your lunch. Give thanks to all of these human beings.

Wait! Don't just lump these individuals together, giving them one big thank you and then rushing on to the next part of "Deli Dance." Meticulously, slowly, go through the list of people. Conjure up in your mind a picture of *each* person. Thank him or her personally, taking a deep breath in and out as you do so. If you're really clever—as I know you are—your list could easily include 200 individuals.

Worried that this will slow you down? Secretly yearn to inhale your food at breakneck speed? First, you can go through this list as you're twiddling your thumbs, waiting for your order to arrive. Guess what? The delay will seem less onerous. You'll be occupied, not champing at the bit, muttering, "What's wrong with the waiter?"

Second, it would be a fine thing for you to eat a trifle—just a smidgen—more slowly. Gulping down your food assures that this afternoon you'll be as sluggish as a python that's just swallowed a forty-pound pig. If you eat fast, you'll eat more. Slow down, and you'll eat less. Extra food in your gut equals more blood rushing to the belly. Less blood available to fuel your brain. Less brainpower to impress Oprah Winfrey during the conference call this afternoon. And if I may gently suggest, you just might find the luncheon experience more pleasurable if you weren't gulping your food.

So take your time with graciously thanking all those hard working folk. Having a grilled cheese sandwich with bacon? A tofu and curry stew? A yogurt, cucumber, and red pepper salad? Come up with your own list of the amazing panorama of living, breathing humans who made today's food. You may find your roll call of twenty takes you right through your meal. If so, you can do the next part of "Deli Dance" at lunch tomorrow. Or go for it now.

Focus on some of the natural resources that made possible your repast. The sun. Its warm rays nourished the lettuce plant. Good old sun. For centuries humans worshipped its regular rising and setting. (And became truly petrified during its occasional eclipses.) Of late humans have gotten a bit casual. We tend to take it for granted. In the clamor of a midtown coffee shop, with dishes clanking, waiters shouting, and a cash register ringing, thinking of nature, any part of nature, can be challenging.

Cast your eyes out the deli's plate-glass windows. Look at the bars of sunlight falling across the street. The glints of light reflecting off the chrome on a limousine cruising by. The brilliant yellow-green of leaves backlit by the sun's rays. Neat, eh? Without this fiery ball ninety-three million miles from the earth, our planet would be one cold, uninhabitable hunk of rock. No lettuce, no bread, no tuna. No humans. *Nada.*

What about the ocean teeming with life, the billions of plankton paddling and pulsating around the sea? These ubiquitous critters, some the size of a grain of rice, some invisible to the eye, some transparent as glass, others iridescent pink or blue, are tasty tidbits for small fry. They, in turn, are fodder for small fish, which are eaten by bigger fish. And bigger fish. Along comes your tuna and—gulp.

Without those wiggling plankton, your tuna would not have had a chance. Send some appreciation to all the flora and fauna of the ocean that helped create your lunch.

It's a privilege to be at the top of the food chain. Enjoy it for a few more moments before returning to your office.

esc

# At the Post Office: Balancing Act

Instant communication via the Internet, faxes, overnight deliveries. You're used to fleet service. A visit to ye olde post office can feel like the rack. Try a balancing act. (Wearing heels? You can't do this one. Proceed to another chapter.) Put any packages down onto the floor. As the line moves forward, you'll come out of your balancing act and shove them along on the floor with your foot.

Come into the Mountain Pose (see page 68 to review). Take several long, deep breaths and start elongating your spine and back muscles. Look straight ahead, softening your gaze. Relax your facial muscles. Take a moment to get very focused. Become as focused as Phillipe Petit before a tight-rope act. He's the Frenchman who, in 1974, danced across high-tension wires strung at a height of 1,350 feet between the World Trade Center twin towers. Petit set a world record, left normally blasé urban residents below cheering, and got arrested for his unauthorized feat! Not to worry. You won't get arrested. Neither will you set any records.

Here's how to get focused: One, find a spot on the floor about twelve feet in front of you, or find a spot on the wall. Keep your eyes gently focused on this spot throughout your practice of this technique. Let it be a spot and not some text on a poster or advertisement. Two, start following your breath. Quietly watch your inhale and exhale. Neutrally observe the pattern of your breath. Three, go for your balancing act.

Start with your feet about hip-width apart. *Slowly* shift some of your weight over onto your left foot. (I suggest your left foot because I'm assuming you're right-handed. If you are, your left leg usually will be dominant and, therefore, stronger. Easier to balance on. Left-handed? Start on your right leg. Ambidextrous? Go for either leg!) To repeat: Shift your weight over slowly. If you hurry at the beginning of this pose, for sure you'll lose your balance later!

Initially keep the other foot on the floor. Start elongating upward from your left ankle. Feel the sense of lengthening traveling up the leg and into your back. Stretch up through the front and back of your torso. Feel your neck becoming longer. Stretch up like a giraffe on the African plain going for a succulent thorn-tree leaf.

Next, check your alignment. Imagine dropping a plumb line from your earlobe down to your feet. Looking at your body *from the side*, the plumb line would pass through the center of your shoulder, hip, and knee, and end up a little bit in front of your ankle. See if you can become aware of your alignment without rushing to judgment about your bad posture. That anxious nattering is an old tape that's better ignored. (Probably it's from a supercritical gym teacher or overly zealous parent.)

Now bring *all* of your weight onto your left leg. As you transfer the weight, keep elongating your spine upward. Notice if your left hip sags out to the left. Lengthen up through the back to help keep your hips squarely facing forward. Gradually, when you're ready, slowly lift the right foot a tiny distance off the floor—at most two or three inches. Take all the time in the world for this. Only lift the foot when you feel rock solid in the other leg. Let the knee of the lifted leg bend slightly. Keep breathing. Beginning to wobble? Let yourself wobble. If need be you can temporarily bring the bent leg down onto the floor to stabilize yourself. Then return to balancing.

Practice detaching yourself from what's going on around you. The clerk seems unusually slow at window 3? Neutrally comment to yourself something like, "Oh, a slow clerk." Immediately return your attention to what counts: stretching up through your leg and back. Woman in front of you muttering about the poor service? Acknowledge to yourself *her* agitation. Even send her some compassion for *her* upset, then withdraw your attention. It's almost as if you were seeing the things around you out of the corner of your eyes—with peripheral vision. Stuff is there, but it's of no consequence to you right now.

When you first start practicing this, you may find yourself getting impatient. "Why am I doing this?" Why *are* you doing this? Certainly *not* to learn how to balance. You're not interested in becoming a high-wire artist or circus performer. You're doing this because balancing is an art that focuses your mind. The trick to balancing is concentration. Yes, it requires a limited amount of muscle control, some physical adeptness. Mostly it's mental focus. The ticket to success is a laser-beam, what meditators call "one-pointed" attention of your mind.

Your mind is off in Timbuktu? Your balancing act will be a falling act. (Luckily, the floor is only two inches away from the lifted foot.) Your brain is jumping off to listen to the postal clerk? You'll start to teeter. As a balancing neophyte, you'll be flooded with nudgy thoughts. Perhaps you'll attribute your first few failures to a genetic defect: "No one in my family could stand on one leg." Or a personal fault: "My balance is terrible."

*Of course* you can't balance on the first try, unless you're a champion tai chi, yoga, or martial arts practitioner. Stick with it. Keep practicing. Keep breathing. Patiently draw your unruly mind back to this moment. Self-critical messages about failure flooding your brain? Calmly observe them and let them go.

Notice what happens when your mind is sharply and clearly focused on the task at hand. Bingo! You can't worry about the line, the postal clerk, the inefficiencies of the mail service, the stock market, or your ill mother-in-law. Your mind is too full of thinking about lengthening up from the ankle, stretching through the back muscles, elongating the neck. And all the while breathing long, deep breaths!

This exercise is an opportunity for you to transform the current moment. To shift the ordinary—standing in a line—into an intriguing experience. Rest assured, anybody can learn to balance. Yes, you may continue to teeter a bit. You may put your foot down a couple of times.

Not that there's any harm in wobbling; in fact, it's healthy for the feet and ankles. When you wobble, all the little bones, muscles, and ligaments in the foot and ankle move gently. The benefits? The lubricating agent, called synovial fluid, squishes around the cushioning cartilage between bones. As a result, the joint is healthier.

As you'll discover, balancing *is* fascinating. (You'll never be bored at the post office again.) Once you've mastered it? You'll have one more arrow in your quiver of physical skills. Far more valuable: This slightly silly physical act translates into emotional and mental balance. You're not as easily thrown. You can't be pushed over by a feather. That pokey customer at the window is a good example. A moment ago he was driving you nuts, studying the design of every available stamp with the fussiness of an art historian examining a newly discovered Rembrandt. Now you don't care.

Need an image of a successful balancer? Call to mind an elegant blue heron, standing on one leg in the shallows of a pond. Waiting for dinner to swim by. Supremely alert. Totally still.

## Are You Atlas? Giving Your Shoulders and Back a Break

Carrying the world on your shoulders? 'Fess up. You're not Atlas, and you're simply not equipped to lug around all the planet's—or your office's—problems. Time to give yourself, your shoulders and back a relaxing stretch.

These are stretches you'll do while seated. Your chair is on casters? Make sure it is stable by pushing it back firmly against a wall or cabinet. Position your buttocks so they are slightly away from the back of your seat, maybe four or five inches. Now take a couple of nice, long breaths. Start *gently* curling and uncurling the spine. Slump down in your seat and round your upper and lower back. Take advantage of this moment. I'm always saying, "Elongate the spine." Now's your chance to slouch like a petulant adolescent.

Caution: Do you have severe pain in your back? A sharp pain shooting down the back of your leg or any neurological symptoms, such as numbness or weakness in your foot or leg? Consult a doctor before doing *any* back stretches.

Not in the above category? Really slump down so that your chest is caved in. Round your shoulders and tilt your head forward. Let your chin tuck down toward the chest. Take a few deep breaths. Then start uncurling the spine. Elongate upward. See if you can begin the elongation in the lower back. Let the lengthening flow into the middle and upper back.

Now lift the head and chin so that your eyes are gazing at a point about midway up the wall in front of you. Don't tilt your head so far back that your neck feels strained. Looking at the ceiling? You've lifted the chin too high. Slightly arch the upper back and gently draw the shoulders back. Please, no harsh or forced movements. Allow the stretch to be subtle. Breathe.

The stretch is so simple it'll be easy for your mind to wander off. A phone is ringing? A coworker laughing? You'll want to answer the phone or hear the joke. Resist that temptation. Keep drawing your attention back to focus on the physical sensations in your back. Notice how in some places your back feels stiff, in others more flexible. Observe how the vertebrae move. Are they moving singly? Or in clumps? As you're noticing, see if you can avoid making any judgments. Just observe the amazing intricacy and complexity of your spine.

You're so used to hurrying through the day's tasks, you'll also be tempted to rush through this stretch. Remember, this is only going to take two or three minutes! Give yourself the gift of a slow stretch. Do the sequence several times. Move elegantly. Languorously.

What's great about this stretch is it gives your spinal disks a refreshing break. Why do your disks need a break? Let's take a moment to look at the anatomy of the disk. These are tough, thick pads of cartilage in between the vertebrae. They consist of an outer ring that is tough and elastic, and a center that is gelatinlike, soft and pulpy. The disks occupy a lot of space—all together they account for about one-quarter of the length of the spinal column. Their function? They separate the vertebrae and provide cushioning and shock absorption for the spine. Without them, bone would be in contact with bone. Very painful and virtually impossible to move!

*All* of the movement in the spine takes places in the disks. It's healthy to move the spine in different directions so as to produce motion within the disks. When you round your back forward, the front side of the disk is compressed or squished down. When you extend and arch the back, the back side is squished. Since most of us have a habit of sitting and standing in one position, the disks are typically compressed more on one side.

You've heard of the condition called "slipped disks." It's a misleading term; there really is no such thing. A disk is not like a poker chip that can skid onto the floor. They do *not* slip or fall out of place. Disk cartilage is firmly *attached* to the vertebrae. But the shape of disks can be deformed, and that's where the trouble starts. Whenever the spine is not moved enough or the disks are compressed consistently in one direction, the disks may start to bulge or herniate, sometimes pressing painfully on surrounding structures.

The best way to keep your vertebrae and spinal disks healthy is to move them gently—and regularly. So it's good idea to do the curl-and-uncurl sequence several times throughout the day. Your spine will be deeply grateful for the favor!

Now add some shoulder stretches. Lift your shoulders high up toward your ears. Then drop them down. As you lift the shoulders, take a long inhale of breath. As you relax the shoulders, exhale fully. Repeat two or three times.

Finally go for some shoulder rolls. Draw your shoulders up toward your ears, then rotate them back toward the wall behind you. Drop the shoulders down. Next roll them forward. Breathe throughout this sequence. Up, back, down, and forward. Keep your head generally erect and looking forward, but let your upper torso get into the action. (As you do this movement, your back will alternate arching and rounding slightly.) Allow the movement to be smooth and fluid.

Notice if you're tightening in your neck or jaw. Relax in these areas. Now reverse the motion. Take your shoulder circles in the opposite direction. Let this be an opportunity to explore your range of motion. Make the circumference of your circle as large and generous as you can. And, of course, keep breathing. Repeat several times in each direction.

Give your shoulders and spine the gift of these stretches *whenever* you're stuck in a chair. Sitting in a traffic jam. Waiting in a doctor's office. On a train. Or at home. Are you someone who, after a hard day at the office, zones out watching TV? When the program gets tedious, spice it up with this easy sequence.

# Before Meeting With Your "Boss": Becoming Rooted

Your supervisor calls you on the intercom. She wants to see you in five, and she didn't sound happy. You don't know what the meeting is about. You feel panicky. Time to become rooted.

Come into the Egyptian Pose. Start long, deep breaths. Uncross your legs, place both feet on the floor, and start gently elongating the spine upward. Relax the shoulders, neck, and face. Take two or three full breaths.

Become aware of your feet. Sense them inside your shoes. If your shoes are not too tight, wiggle your toes around. (If you're wearing tight pumps and can quickly slip them off, do so.) Feel your toes moving inside your socks or stockings. Now press down equally with each foot. Experience your toes, balls, and heels firmly connected to the carpet, tile, or wood floor beneath you.

Next start imagining roots descending from the soles of your feet. Feel your roots dropping through the floor. Whether your office is on the thirty-fourth floor or the second, your imaginary roots burrow down through poured concrete, marble imported from Italy, and steel girders. Down, down through all the intervening floors. Past accounting and personnel, past the murals in the ground-floor lobby, past the freight elevators, roots plunging into the rich soil beneath the building.

Visualize your roots penetrating deep, branching out, traveling beneath adjacent parking lots. They slither under delivery vans, crowded sidewalks, and pyramids of oranges stacked at the corner deli.

As your roots extend and stretch underground, you start feeling more stable. Grounded. Keep breathing. Long, deep breaths. Continue gently stretching your spine upward, relaxing your neck, jaw, and facial muscles.

A root is tough—and persistent. An obstacle in its path? The root makes a detour. It finds the cracks in concrete foundations, slithers around boulders. If need be, it splits rocks wide open. Imagine your own roots serenely negotiating around any obstructions.

Once a tree is full grown, it has astounding stability. If a sixty-mile-per-hour wind is tossing the branches of a giant oak, the roots stay rooted, shifting slightly in the soil. Let a sense of how strong your own roots are come into your being. No matter what your manager says today, you're not going to be blown over. See yourself in the meeting steady and calm. You'll breathe and stand—or more likely—sit your ground.

Now bring your consciousness back to the sensations in your feet. Feel your arches, the balls of your feet, your toes. Scrunch up your toes. If you're in your socks or stockings, alternate scrunching up your toes, then spreading them widely. Do this a couple of times. Then return to an awareness of your feet planted solidly on the floor.

Make a promise to yourself *in advance* of your meeting: Even if your supervisor is critical of you, you'll give yourself some of the positive feedback she can't. You'll give yourself some pats on the back for the many things you've done right.

Roots are flexible. Their courses are never predictable. Underground roots grow straight, zigzag, meander in long circles, curve around stones, or plunge straight down. Breathe. You too will be flexible in your meeting with your boss. Ready to stand firm when appropriate, to make a deviation from your planned course when necessary.

Give yourself a mini pep talk. You got this job for a reason. You're smart, competent, creative. You like people. You're great with computers. You love math. Whatever your talents are, they resulted in your being hired. Those talents are deep inside you, ready to support and sustain you.

And remember, your employer *is* a human being—with the foibles we all share and plenty of good stuff. Like a vulnerable heart thumping away. She or he has friends, family, a daughter, a nephew, some special individuals she loves dearly and who love her too.

You have a tendency to think of your manager as a "boss"? Perhaps your name for her is even more extreme? "Slime" or worse? You might consider changing how you refer to her, both in your private thoughts and complaining sessions with friends. She's an employer, a manager, or an administrator. It will make you think of her more neutrally. Less like Simon Legree, the slave driver in *Uncle Tom's Cabin*. If she's not a slave driver, presto, you're not a slave.

Good luck with your meeting. By the way, don't forget to put your shoes back on!

Suggested session for at home: If you practice your sense of rootedness at a less pressured time, then the next time the heat is on, you'll be better prepared. Do you have a favorite tree? A big pine tree in your backyard? A beautiful magnolia on a neighbor's lawn? A tough ginkgo on the street? Spend some time studying this tree the next time you get a chance.

Appreciate its amazingly resilient and strong roots. A tree's roots stretch as far underground as the canopy of branches extends up to the sky. You're an urban dweller?

Your street-wise tree will have roots that do not have the luxury of extending out so far. But these roots are equally amazing: poking down through asphalt, snaking past water mains and gas lines. Be aware of the accomplishments of whichever tree you select. How it's weathered droughts, blizzards, and lightning strikes. Allow a little awe to seep into your heart.

Let some of the tree's emphatic, firm rootedness come into your being.

esc

# Rush-Hour Relief: By Bus, Subway, and Foot

# What's the Hurry? How to Walk Through the Subway Turnstile Slowly

Admit it! You don't have an important meeting with the President of CBS. Nor are you meeting a movie star for lunch. (Even if you did, it would be better to arrive at the meeting calm and refreshed, instead of red-faced and sweaty.) Yet you're still racing down the subway steps. What would happen if, for once, you walked slowly, impeccably slowly, through the turnstile?

The trick to walking at a laggard's pace through turnstiles is to prepare yourself in advance. On the day in which you do this exercise, leave your home five to six minutes early. You may protest, "I don't need five minutes to walk through a turnstile." You're right, you don't. But stay with me and you'll see why you may need those extra five.

If you're in the habit of running down the subway steps, a sluggish stride will not be easy. As you approach the station, imagine a flashing red light. Slow down. You might even repeat to yourself, "I'm going to walk calmly." " I'm going to dawdle and linger." "I'm going to creep."

As you get closer to the station, you see a swarm of humanity pushing and shoving into the station. Soon this horde is behind you, in front of you. On your left and right sides, people are rushing pell-mell down the steps. Continue to loll along at a slothlike pace.

Quite possibly someone will cast you a dirty look and mutter, "Get a move on." Breathe. Continue at a sedate, *adagio* pace down the steps. Walk means walk. Do not allow yourself to be infected by the adrenaline rush around you.

Resist the temptation to run. This is exquisitely hard when people are streaking past you. Ignore the comments, the frowns, the contagion of dashing. Breathe and stay with your own pace. If need be, imagine yourself on crutches, your leg in a cast. For reasons of safety, you must move at a snail's pace.

Does this task seem impossible? As you're leisurely sauntering down the steps, breathe and give yourself a distraction. Consider some of the major accomplishments of your life. You survived eighteen hours of labor bringing forth your miraculous son. You paid off your student loans. Last month you may have gone rollerblading, jumped off a bridge with bungee cords strapped to your waist, or spoken to your mother-in-law for the first time in three years. It's amazing the things you do. This small task you can also accomplish.

Okay, so you're at the bottom of the steps. Breathe. You're within a few feet of the turnstile. Breathe again. Continue walking at your regal, deliberate pace. You're at the turnstile. A train is rumbling into the station. Remember the extra five minutes you allowed yourself this morning? This is the moment to take advantage of that extra time. Keep strolling at your measured, unflustered pace.

Yes, I know this is hard. All of your ingrained habits say, "Run!" Yes, you may miss this train. Yes, this could be the last subway until 2010. Yes, an irate person may be breathing down your neck. Calmly step to one side and let him pass. If he wants to break his neck sprinting for the subway, that's his affair.

Pause at the turnstile. Take one breath in and one breath out. Feel like the longest breath in the world? Now pass through the turnstile. You did it! Now you can march briskly to the train. The funny thing is, you may not feel like doing so. You might just want to saunter. To amble or mosey as you enjoy the bizarre sight of your fellow commuters scurrying in all directions.

Practice lounging through the turnstile a few more times before you graduate to this advanced exercise: Get ready to proceed slowly and calmly through the turnstile, imagining some incredibly precious and unique package clasped in your arms. This could be a sleeping infant, maybe your brilliant and beautiful four-month-old son. Perhaps the baby Martin Luther King, the infant Ella Fitzgerald. Or Beethoven as a toddler. What a loss to the world if you dropped your valuable cargo!

What about a stack of Wedgwood teacups or a Tiffany lamp? Those delicate, fragile cups are balanced precariously one on top of another. They're clattering noisily. One false move and they crash into a thousand shards. Are you going to hurry? No. Do you care if the person behind you is making odd, choking sounds remarkably similar to growls? No. All that is important is to get through the turnstile gracefully and calmly—without disturbing your treasured cargo.

Beautiful. Life on the subway will never be the same again.

Note: If this feels too hard to do on a regular workday, try it first on a weekend. (Or whatever day you have off.) Once you have honed your sauntering skills, graduate to the rush-hour bedlam.

## Cell-Phone Mania: Practicing Detachment

"Hi, it's George."
"I'm at Michigan and Randolph."
"I called Dotty. Guess what she said? She loved it!"
*Said in a much louder voice,* "She adored it. I never . . ."

The litany of trivia blasts into your consciousness, making it impossible for you to read or think. Since their introduction a few years ago, cell phones seem to be ubiquitous. Indeed, an estimated 100 million or more dot the land. Clearly, they're here to stay; they're too darned convenient for people to give them up.

So how can you find a little peace while being an unwilling eavesdropper as George gabs to Sal? Start with the usual: long, deep breaths. In different sections of this book, you've read the words, "Breathe long, deep breaths," many times. By now your eye may just flick right over the words and dart on to the next phrase. Hold it! Really *do* breathe, a nice generous inhale and exhale.

Now to practice *detaching* from the irritant at hand. There are a couple of ways to do this. First, become aware of your judgments about the offending party. Yes, his conversation seems remarkably trivial. Step back for a moment. What percentage of your own conversations are also taken up by what a third party might designate as "trivia"? "Wow! It's humid today!" "Shall we order in Chinese or Thai?" "Did you see those nose rings?" Most of the time we aren't discussing Proust or the state of the Russian economy.

Often one woman's trivia is another's vital statistics. It might be that the Dotty you heard the cell-phone user referring to was waxing ecstatic about a new motorized wheelchair. Hardly an insignificant matter to Dotty. And you yourself may not consider whether you eat Chinese or Thai inconsequential either, particularly if you have an allergy to MSG.

Besides, isn't the exchange of minutiae, which we might call the exchange of unimportant civilities, necessary to human society? The glue that keeps us connected to one another? These superficial exchanges are reassuring, soothing. They remind us that we're all humans bouncing about in the same boat. What would we do without the trivia of talking about the weather? Without the bond of "Beautiful day, isn't it?"

Perhaps the near-continuous refrain of human chit-chat is a bit like the grooming monkeys do. Animal behaviorists have long asserted that the frequent tactile contact, the hand stroking through hair, the physical closeness of inspecting for lice keeps a tribe of monkeys in a state of equilibrium. It's an activity that increases social cohesiveness.

You may object, "Whether casual chatting is good for society or not, it's decidedly bad for me when it's two feet away and noisily invading my personal space." Good point. Breathe and bring your mind back to focus on detaching from this particular cell-phone nuisance.

A second technique that may help: Instead of single-mindedly focusing on the irritant, shift your attention to other stimuli around you. Riding on a bus or train? Lift your eyes to the passing scene outside the window. Notice the light filtering through the leaves of the trees. Check out the man skillfully painting the sidewalk with chalk. From your vantage point it looks like an intriguing portrait. A copy of a Michelangelo?

Become aware of other non-cell-phone sounds around you. A couple of teenagers giggling. The rustle of a newspaper. The conductor's voice.

With each sight or sound, see if you can observe without rushing to judgment. Simply notice. Practice being aware of the stimuli around you as an *abstract* texture of sights and sounds. A whole cloth of experience in which nothing in particular stands out.

Suppose one Sunday you drove up to a cabin in the woods. You're sitting quietly on a dock quietly enjoying the view of a still, calm lake—one without motorboats or skis. What would you notice? Perhaps a dark mass of pine trees around the water's edge. Maybe puffs of creamy white clouds in the sky. Reflections of clouds and trees in the water. Ripples on the surface of water as a slight breeze crosses the lake. The slate blue and black color of the water.

Unless you're a poet or a painter, you probably wouldn't single out an individual pine tree to focus on. In your laid-back state, you accept the landscape without getting into any judgments. You don't pick one cloud as a superior cloud. You don't judge a particular ripple as better than or worse than another. It's the overall image that has you enthralled. The totality of the scene sends you into a peaceful state.

I'm not saying the bus going down Michigan Street in Chicago is ever going to be like a crystal-clear lake in New Hampshire. But you can make a decision to see the whole. To see it more neutrally. "Hmmm. Here I am riding on a bus." Try on a more distant perspective, almost as if you were looking at the scene through the reverse end of a telescope. "Ahhh, yes. A voice speaking. A motor humming. Twenty-first-century sights and sounds. And there's me observing." Keep breathing.

You yourself are a cell-phone user? You might stop and think the next time you're on the verge of making a call. "Can I wait until I'm off the bus?" "How is my action going to impact others around me?" "Could I speak in a lower voice?" Consider turning *off* your phone when you're in close quarters with others, such as on public transportation or in a restaurant.

esc

# The Chill-Out:
# Going into a Mini-Hibernation

Is your life sometimes like a hummingbird's? All day long you speed from task to task. Never stopping. Eating on the run.

At their most feverish moments, the tiny hearts of hummingbirds are beating at about 615 times per minute. Unlike other birds, these diminutive creatures seldom hop or walk. How do they have the energy to keep going? At night, they rest. *Really* rest. Their metabolism takes a dive. They drop off to sleep and their temperature plummets from a high of 115°F to around 55°F.

It's called a mini-hibernation. Next day, they wake refreshed, ready to flit from morning glory to morning glory. You can do a mini-hibernation, too: right now, sitting on this bus or subway. After all, every night you have practice. When you fall asleep at night, your body's metabolic rate also drops. Muscles relax, body temperature goes down, heart rate decreases, pulse rate dips, breathing slows. Even your brain waves shift to a more sedate pace. In the first moments of drifting off to sleep, a brain-wave pattern called beta predominates. It gives way to alpha, theta, and delta patterns, even slower brain waves.

Throughout the night, you cycle in and out of various sleep stages that help to enhance your immune system and replenish muscular energy. In a sense, your batteries are recharged.

Charge up your batteries right now on this subway or bus by helping your hummingbird metabolism to slow down. Come into the Egyptian Pose and start long, deep breaths. You can do this calming technique with your eyes open or closed. If you choose to keep your eyes open, keep them unfocused. Avoid looking directly at people or written words.

This is a counting breath. As you breathe, you count. You'll count one on the inhale, hold the breath for four counts, then exhale for a count of two. Repeat. Keep repeating. Stay aware of what's happening in your body as you do this. It's easy to hike up your shoulders or tense in your chest as you hold your breath. Let the holding be easy, gentle. See if you can relax shoulders, neck, jaw as you hold. Let your torso feel like it's floating above your hips.

Holding for four counts seems to be too long? If you seem to be running out of breath, change the count. Initially, hold for just two counts. Inhale one count, hold two counts, exhale two counts. If it feels like you could hold the breath longer, go for 2:8:4. Keep going for three to five rounds. Then return to normal breathing. Breathe normally for a few counts then return to the 1:4:2 breath or whichever version you're doing.

At once, you'll notice how easy it is to fall off the count. Expect your mind to wander off. "What's for supper?" "I detest that guy's socks." When these distracting thoughts pop up, notice them and then gently draw your mind back to focus on the count. You'll also notice self-judging thoughts plaguing your brain: "I can't do this." "It's making me more stressed, not less."

All of these thoughts are perfectly *normal*. You're not a bad or a hopeless case. Your mind is unruly like everybody else's in the world. It's almost as if your thought patterns are like a rambunctious puppy exploring every crack in the pavement. You just need to practice gently coaxing your rowdy puppy-mind back by your side.

One way to rein in your thoughts: Keep returning to an awareness of the physical sensation of the slight movements in your body as you breathe. Feel your belly rising and falling. Notice the slight expansion and contraction of your ribs. Listen to the soft purring sound your breath makes inside your throat.

Why not just doze off or nap?

One, sleeping on a public conveyance is risky. Obviously, nodding off puts you in a highly vulnerable state. You could miss your stop or be oblivious to a pickpocket slipping your wallet out of your jacket. When you're doing the 1:4:2 breath, you're fully awake and alert.

Two, you tend to be confused and groggy after a nap. You're prone to forgetfulness and accidents. Your slightly muddled state could jeopardize the safety of your walk home from the subway or bus.

Mainly, you'll just feel better. Calm body, calm mind. After you've nudged your whole physiology into a mini-hibernation, you'll be ready for what's next on the agenda. Keen for a romp with your collie. Ready to fix supper for a friend. Up for helping your daughter with her chemistry homework. Prepared to plant petunias in your window boxes.

For a wonderful compendium of breathing exercises and relaxation and coping skills, check out the *Relaxation and Stress Reduction Workbook* by Martha Davis, Elizabeth Eshelman, and Matthew McKay. One of the best breathing tape cassettes? *Breathing, the Master Key to Self Healing* by Dr. Andrew Weil.

esc

# Symphony of the Neck:
# Gentle Neck Stretches

Let's face it. Life can be a pain in the neck. No wonder. We're lugging around a passel of heavy skull bones, plus all those complex, convoluted folds of gray matter. Typically, this package weighs ten to twelve pounds. By the way, don't be disheartened if your head, *ergo* your brain, is small. So was Einstein's. Our brainpower is measured by the number of neuron connections, not by size.

Usually we lug around this precious cargo as casually as if it were a wet bathing suit. For example, notice how your neighbors on this particular train, bus, or subway are sitting right now. I bet they're slumped back in their seats, shoulders rounded, heads thrust forward.

And now take a look at yourself: You, too, are probably in said slumped position. If you are, the weight of your mighty skull and profound, IQ-loaded brain is not being supported by the spinal column but instead by the muscles of the neck. Definitely a recipe for neck strain.

So let's experiment. Come into the Egyptian Pose. Start sending messages from your brain to the muscles in the back that lift the spine. Let the spine gently elongate. Think of your spine as starting at the tailbone and rising up all the way to the base of the skull.

See if you can position your head and neck so that you are neither jutting your head and jaw forward nor tightly tucking your chin in and down. The vertebrae in the neck should be comfortably and naturally aligned with those in your back. They're not broken at the shoulders like one of those frozen rose buds whose stems do a U-turn and blossoms drop, as soon as they leave the florist.

At first this alignment of your head and neck may feel odd. It figures. You've probably been sitting with shoulders slightly rounded and chin forward for most of your life. Yet you may be unaware what impact this position has on the rest of your body. To check this out, deliberately let your head come forward, and round your shoulders. Feel how that caves in your chest and rounds the lower spine. Then gently elongate the spine and draw the head back slightly. Lift the chin so it's horizontal to the floor. Become aware of the chest opening and lifting.

Try the slump again. Notice how when the head is thrust forward it makes your ribs cave in, making it difficult to get a full, deep breath. Elongate up again. Now, at the same time, you're gently drawing your head and neck into alignment with the back, elongating up through the muscles in the neck. This motion is very subtle. See if you can elongate upward without hunching up or tightening your shoulders. Lengthen upward without making the back of the neck rigid. Let the neck maintain its natural, concave curve.

Do all of the above, while remembering to breathe. Relax the jaw muscles. Relax the muscles around the mouth and eyes. See if you can lift the crown or top of your head a tiny bit higher. Imagine your head reaching up toward the ceiling of the subway, stretching toward the street, buildings, sun, clouds, and stars above.

So, you're sitting tall. How do you like it? Well, you may not like it. At first, sitting up seems awkward and uncomfortable. Odds are your back muscles are used to slumping. They may protest at waking up, becoming active. And sitting with the chest open and elevated can make you feel vulnerable. Old habits die hard. Stay with it. Breathe.

Next, let's give those overworked, stressed neck muscles of yours a relaxing stretch, while maintaining an elongated back.

Slowly, very slowly, start tilting the head forward, drawing the chin down to the chest. You may say to yourself, "This movement is a cinch." It'll be tempting to do it fast. Resist the temptation. Proceed at a molasses pace, keeping your attention exquisitely focused on the back of your neck.

See if you can feel the vertebrae in the neck, all seven of them, articulate as the head drops forward. Feel the muscles in the back of the neck stretch and lengthen. Here an old habit is apt to raise its ugly head. Your body, long used to slumping, may want to slump. Even though the head is tilted forward, keep lifting up through your back.

Focus on the back of your neck. Imagine breathing deep into the fibers of the muscles; imagine the oxygen being delivered to each cell. Feel the muscles softening and relaxing. With each breath, picture them opening and expanding.

Now shift your consciousness elsewhere in the body. Scan through your shoulders, torso, hips, arms, hands, legs, and feet. Do you notice any constriction or holding? Residual tension? Relax in these places.

Return to your neck. Remember to breathe. Now gradually lift your head up so that your face is looking forward. This sequence is *not* as simple as it seems. Please don't do it mechanically. Remember to do it very slowly. If you breathe throughout and pay exacting attention to each subtle detail, not only will your neck feel better, but also you will arrive at your destination refreshed and calm.

If you're doing "Symphony of the Neck" at the appropriate pace, it should take two to three minutes. Recommended: Do it several times a day.

## Star Gazer: Visiting Outer Space During Rush-Hour Madness

Are you in one of those stop-the-world-I-want-to-get-off moods? Sometimes an escape is just the ticket. You can escape into one of your favorite mystery thrillers—or escape into the mysteries of the universe.

Come into either the Egyptian Pose or the Mountain Pose. Start long, deep breaths; elongate the spine; relax the neck, shoulders, and jaw. Either gently close your eyes or keep them open with a soft, unfocused gaze.

Here you are deep underground, tunneling beneath rocks and soil. Imagine that you can see up to the sky above. Laser-beam your sight up through the metal of the subway roof, up through the concrete tunnel through which you're being swiftly or slowly (depending upon the whims of your friendly transit company) propelled. Let your gaze pass through the dense maze of electrical wiring, water and gas mains, asphalt and pavement above your head.

Take your mind up through the city streets, up past the skyscrapers, up into the air above the city. Keep going. Up beyond the height at which birds migrate (2,500 feet), up above the communication satellites whizzing overhead (22,280 miles above the equator).

Imagine feasting your eyes on the stars. Yes, they're up there. No matter if the city is socked in with smog, fog, or snow. No matter if sheets of rain are drenching the sidewalks above your head. It's just a temporary atmospheric disturbance; a blip in what's called the troposphere, the place where most clouds and what we humans call "weather" hang out.

Let your mind soar up beyond the troposphere, up the seven miles to the stratosphere. Here there's no water vapor, no dust, no pollution to cloud your vision. Start letting a sense of spaciousness and wonder enter your being.

Continue to breathe. Relax the shoulders. Elongate the spine upward.

In the midst of our daily dramas, we forget the cosmos out there. No matter if it's daytime—the stars are there. Brilliantly shining. Trillions of whirling balls of hot gas, all generating intense light and unimaginable heat. Stars burning and burning—for millions of years. Old stars and young stars, some cooling down, glowing like dying embers. Others exploding into supernovae that show up on sophisticated satellite cameras as bursts of brilliant red, green, purple.

It's easy to forget that what we think of as "our" sun is just another star. Having the diameter of about 109 earths, it seems enormous. And it's hot: 9,900 degrees Fahrenheit. Although we have a particular interest in our sun, it's a rather common, ordinary star, one among billions of stars in the Milky Way. In fact, no bigger, no smaller, no brighter, no dimmer than innumerable other stars. (It seems particularly big because it's closer to Earth than any of the other stars.)

Hearing the screech of iron wheels against iron rails? Feeling the lurching of your subway car? Keep breathing.

Ponder the galaxies, those islands of whirling stars. A typical large galaxy has 100 billion stars. A small one has a paltry few hundred thousand stars. Not too long ago, humans thought that the Milky Way was the only galaxy in the universe. Not true. Now we know there are billions of other galaxies with exotic names like Andromeda, Whirlpool, Centaurus A, and Pinwheel.

Contemplate the planets. Once every school child knew there were a total of nine planets, including the earth, orbiting around our sun. With new twenty-first-century refinements in telescopes, spectrometers, and advanced search techniques, more and more planets *outside* our solar system are being detected. The total number of planets is up to forty-six and growing. This form of research is called extrasolar planetary exploration, and it promises to explode current notions of the universe.

Keep breathing. End your subway visit to the starry universe by focusing on the Big Bang. That's the theory, currently dominant among astronomers, that the universe started in a big explosion of whirling fire. From that moment billions of years ago, the universe has been expanding. Stars and galaxies are streaking out into space, away from one another. Who knows if this theory will be proven or disproven by the astronomers of the twenty-first century?

In the meantime, there's nothing like the dazzling brilliance of the universe to give us a little perspective on our personal problems. Maybe they're not so big! Some of your problems might even start to look quite miniscule.

Don't limit this mental exercise to underground voyages. Also do it while above ground and in broad daylight. When you're caught in a traffic jam, stopped at a red light, or waiting for a bus, it's nifty to look up at the sky and imagine the stars brightly shining above the blue sky, cloud cover, or snow.

To help prepare, take some time out on a clear evening to stand at a window in your apartment or house. Enjoy the incredible panorama of the night sky. Or visit the Internet. The NASA Web site is packed with tantalizing information about (and stunning photographs of) supernovae, black holes, and pulsars.

## Straphanger Special: A Relaxing Twist

As the bus pulls into the stop where you're not-so-patiently waiting, you groan. It's standing room only. You've been hunched over your computer all day typing spreadsheets and now you're exhausted and crabby. Not having a seat is the last straw. Or is it? You've been sitting in one position all day. Standing on your own two feet and doing the Straphanger Special can actually do wonders after a long day at the office.

This stretch only works if you're *not* packed in like sardines. There must be some space on either side of you and behind you. Ten to twelve inches of clearance on each side will do. Forget your measuring tape? Eyeball it. If you *are* packed in like sardines, turn to the Mountain Pose on page 68.

To begin, place your feet hip-width apart and bend the knees slightly. Keep the knees bent *throughout* the exercise. You'll be more stable with bent knees, so if the bus suddenly stops or swerves, your body will gently rock with the motion and you'll be able to keep your balance without lurching into your neighbors. (Keeping your balance while wearing high heels is, of course, more tricky. You might consider changing into running shoes for your commute to and from the office.)

Reach up with your right arm to hold on to the strap or metal bar above you. Elongate the spine. Relax your face and jaw. Breathe deep into the belly. Check to see that the lifted shoulder, your right shoulder, is relaxed. This can feel like a bit of a paradox. While stretching the shoulder and arm on the right side upward, imagine sending your breath into the muscles on that side of the body. Feel the muscles opening and expanding.

Carrying a pocketbook? Let it hang from the raised shoulder. Toting a briefcase? Place it on the floor between your legs. Let your other arm hang by your side in a relaxed position.

Starting with a gentle and super-slow motion in the waist, begin to turn your torso to the left. Use subtle, microscopic movements, movements so leisurely that a bystander would barely see you moving. Centimeter by centimeter, let your torso gently turn to the side.

Allow the motion to spiral up your spine. As you continue to elongate the spine, let the middle back, upper back, chest, shoulders, neck, and head also turn to your left. Move very slowly. Relax the shoulders, neck, and jaw as you do this. It's almost as if your body were becoming one of those old-fashioned barber signs, with red lines spiraling up a white column.

Breathe. Let this be a delicious stretch. Take a cue from your pet. The world is generally divided into cat owners and dog owners, though some animal lovers adore both species. Whichever category you fall into, imagine your favorite kitty or pooch doing a stretch. Do they huff and puff? Grimace with the strain? Furrow their brows? Murmur to themselves, "No pain, no gain"? No way. They stretch, casually, languorously, deliciously.

As you do the twist, bring a little playful feline or canine energy into your being.

It's most likely that nobody will notice you. If it makes you feel more comfortable, imagine that you are looking behind you to check the phone number of the podiatrist who's been advertising in the bus for centuries or to scan the street signs to identify your specific location.

Look over the left shoulder for a couple of counts. Keep softening the neck muscles. Relax your throat. Check to see that your knees are still slightly bent. Please—no forcing, no straining. This should be a pleasurable streeeeaaatch.

Use your breath to help you come a little deeper into the twist. So how do you use the breath to help you stretch more deeply? On each inhalation, elongate the spine a tiny bit higher—without hunching the shoulders up! On each exhalation, allow the spine to come further into the twist. When you've reached what feels like the fullest twist you can achieve today, take a couple of deep breaths. Then gradually release, slowly unwinding the torso so it faces forward.

What does "the fullest twist you can achieve today" mean? It means paying meticulous attention to how your body *feels* and going only so far into the motion as is comfortable. It means respecting your body and being gentle. This is not a competition. You are not attempting to prove anything to yourself or others. You're not trying to outdo a film star who you saw wrapping her body into a pretzel shape in an advertisement for swimsuits.

Observing how your body feels takes concentration. Stay focused on what you're doing. If you find your mind has zoomed off to listen to two teenagers complaining about their English teacher, bring your awareness back to your body.

Starting to feel strained? Back off. Let your spine unwind, but don't come completely out of the twist. Back off slightly and breathe. After a few nice, long breaths, see if you can go back into the twist, taking your body a little bit further into the stretch. If you experience pain, come out of the position completely. Stand looking forward and do some diaphragmatic breathing.

Once you have completed the Straphanger Special on the left side and are standing with the torso facing forward, take a couple of long breaths. Change arms. Reach up with your left hand to find the hanging strap or metal pole. If you're carrying a pocketbook, switch it over to the left shoulder.

Elongate your spine. Really activate those back muscles to lengthen upward, stretching up both in the lower and upper back. At the same time be sure to keep breathing and to relax the shoulders. Again, check to see that your knees are still slightly bent.

Turn to look over your right shoulder. Again start the motion in your waist, and let the movement gradually rise up into the chest, shoulders, neck, and head. Stay with that delicious feline or canine energy. Keep breathing. Imagine, as you are looking over your shoulder, that you see one of your favorite people sitting in the bus, your gorgeous talented daughter, your brilliant four-year-old niece, your long-lost college roommate.

Call to mind some of the details of that person's face. A freckled nose, long pigtails, a slight gap between the two front teeth when she smiles. Let into your heart some of the fondness, the affection you feel for this special person. Return to face forward. Do this several times on each side.

If someone gets up and a seat becomes available, avoid the knee-jerk, competitive lunge for a parking place for your buttocks. Instead, consider remaining standing and doing the twist a couple more times. Remain standing and you might just feel more sprightly, more alive when you get home.

This gentle twist is also great for the subway or a crowded commuter train. Doing the Straphanger Special on a subway and have your briefcase on the floor between your feet? Be sure to keep your foot or leg in contact with the briefcase so you always know where it is.

Doing this exercise in a location where, instead of straps or poles overhead, there are handles on the back of the seats? Follow the directions above with one small adjustment. Place right arm on the seat handle, then gradually turn to look to your left. And vice versa.

# Underground Compassion: Appreciating the Denizens of the Metro

After a long day at the office, a rude or inconsiderate person can push you over the top. Yet expressing wrath toward the person who just stepped on your toe doesn't help. It was probably an accident anyway.

Let's play with a human emotion often missing on public transportation: compassion. What *is* compassion anyhow? Webster's dictionary says "it's sympathetic consciousness of others' distress." Feeling compassionate is both to be aware of somebody else's experience and to care about their feelings.

Usually we're naturally compassionate toward a member of our family, a close friend, or a child. Your brother doesn't get his promotion? You're disappointed along with him. Goddaughter Suzie breaks her arm? You vicariously experience her pain.

It gets ticklish when the person is a stranger. It's really tough when that stranger is standing right next to you. Let's start with some folk who are not in your line of vision, people whose hard labors make your voyage today possible.

First, come into the Egyptian Pose. Take some long, deep breaths. Or if there is standing room only, come into the Mountain Pose. Take a moment to imagine the existence of subway workers. On any given day or night there'll be hundreds of people laboring molelike beneath the earth.

What would it be like to be in a subterranean world all day long? Five days a week? Year after year? No view of the sky, no lunch-hour spent walking on the sunny side of the street, enjoying the warm rays of a winter sun.

Send some compassion to the station agents trapped in their claustrophobic cubicles. Think of their long, lonely hours. The boredom of perpetually counting out change, the irritation of angry customers who cuss them out.

Direct some thanks to the train operators who stare out into a black tunnel all day or all night long. Think of their primary visual stimuli: red lights turning to amber, amber to green, green to amber and red. Fleetingly, they see other members of the human race standing on a dimly lit platform, then they are submerged again in a dingy gloom.

Not feeling particularly thankful right now? Just want to get home as fast as possible—without thinking about *any-thing*? Turn to "The Chill-Out" on page 113. Once you're feeling calmer, return to this exercise.

Breathe deep into the belly. What about the conduc-tors? They too rattle along in dark cubicles. They are immersed in the tedium of repeating over and over such inspiring words as "Please stand clear of the moving doors." Whenever they stick their heads out of their cubicles they risk being sworn at, punched, or spat upon. (That's why many conductors wear goggles.) Send some consideration and concern to these employees.

Of course the jobs subway workers have will differ, depending upon whether you're riding an old metro system or a more automated and modern one. Tailor your compas-sion exercise accordingly.

Take your compassion meditation one step further. Think of all the laborers who constructed these under-ground tunnels. If you're riding on a subway in Philadel-phia, New York, Chicago, or Boston, the work was backbreaking. It predated the bulldozers, backhoes, and other large earth-moving equipment now commonly used at urban construction sites.

Imagine dynamite blasting tons of bedrock, then laborers sledgehammering giant boulders into smaller rocks. Dirt, sand, and rocks heaved out by buckets. Debris carted off in wheelbarrows and mule-drawn wagons. Rock falls shoveled away, tunnel cave-ins dug out, all by hand. You thought you had back problems sitting at a computer all day! A lot of aching muscles, strained backs, and sweat built the subway you're currently riding.

Speeding along on one of the more recently constructed metros in Atlanta, San Francisco, Los Angeles, or Washington? They too required years of labor. Tunneling under San Francisco Bay under compressed air conditions. Installing the intersecting concrete vaults on the Washington subway. These massive projects, though less back-breaking than earlier ones, still required hard and often hazardous labor. Take a moment to give thanks to all of these workers.

Don't forget to include the city planners, architects, engineers, surveyors, industrial designers, geologists, bankers, politicians, and taxpayers whose combined skills and financial backing put this transportation system on the map.

Once you've gotten adept at practicing compassion underground, go for an above-ground version. Next time you're on a bus or train, send some compassion and thanks to all the workers who make your journey possible.

esc

# Leisurely Stroll:
# The Pluses of Loitering

You've just gotten off a crowded bus, subway, or train. You have a seven-block walk. It's a walk you've done, perhaps, 500 times. You're on automatic pilot. Your mind is focused on getting where you're going—as fast as possible.

Today, practice loitering. "To delay an activity with aimless idle stops and pauses" is Webster's definition of the verb "loiter." Aimless, idle. Words to alarm the average American who's always rushing somewhere. Now I know *you,* at this exact moment, are going somewhere important. You're racing home from the bus stop. Striding to the grocery store. Dashing to the cleaners. Hastening to your parked car.

Remember how often you complain about your car being parked "miles away"? Today, transform that distance from a deficit into a plus. Decide to practice experiencing your walk not as an activity to transport you to the goal of the grocery store, cleaners, or parked car, but as an opportunity to loiter and loaf *in between* here and there.

It's not going to take significantly longer. Let's say it does take a few minutes longer, perhaps three to five minutes. In the scheme of things, does it really matter? In fact, because you'll be intrigued and amused, you may not even notice the time difference.

Before starting on your stroll, take a few long, deep breaths. Bring your mind to focus on this present moment. Fixated on the future? Already imagining yourself drinking the cool drink that is sitting in your fridge at home? You won't be able to see all the new sights between here and there. You may ask, "What new sights?" Indeed, it's not likely you'll find a Parisian cafe with Frenchmen sipping absinthe. Nor will you stumble upon your favorite movie star rehearsing her lines. Chances are there'll be nary a pair of whooping cranes doing their elaborate mating dance.

Yet your route is strewn with fascinating, curious, and funny stuff—flora and fauna that you normally charge by in a state of obliviousness. How can you bring a different awareness into your being?

Sure, you could slog along in a funk. You could drag yourself along on the treadmill of your familiar internal monologue of all the things that are "wrong." Wrong at your job, in this city, or in your life. You could stay mired in anticipation of problems that may await you at home.

Admit it. Isn't it a tad boring? Tediously reminiscent of the summer reruns of TV shows you've already seen twice? As you dawdle along, why not make a decision: With the extra time provided by your loitering, you'll keep your eyes peeled for ordinary things or people along your route that are extraordinary!

What might you see differently, freshly? Here's a sample of common sights that may help you get started: A couple walking down the ramp to an underground parking lot. They appear to be in their fifties? They're holding hands. Every few steps their shoulders touch. They might be about to celebrate a thirtieth wedding anniversary. Or perhaps they just met. Like love-crossed adolescents, they're plunged into the heart-tumbling world of a juicy romance.

A woman trying to comfort a furious baby. The baby is red in the face and hitting the woman's chest with her fists. And screaming. The shrieks go on and on. At first you might think, "What a terrible mother." Then you decide to let go of assumptions. Maybe the woman *is* a bit inexperienced.

After years of unsuccessful fertility treatments, she's in heaven. Big-time. She just returned from Honduras with her already totally beloved, adopted baby. The baby hasn't yet gotten used to her new mother.

Brilliant pink flowers, impatiens, planted at the base of a tree. Someone took the trouble, kneeling in the soil, squatting or bending over, to plant flowers that are purely ornamental. They adorn a public space and make it more pleasant for you and other strangers.

A walk sign at a pedestrian crossing. At times the very idea of an electronic machine telling you when to walk is positively galling. But you forget how nifty it is to live in a community with red lights. Imagine the chaos of an intersection in a busy city like Marrakesh. There cars, bicycles, scooters, trucks, pedestrians (many of whom are children darting every which way), donkeys, camels, goats, all vie for a piece of the dusty roadway. You would literally risk life and limb making your way across the thoroughfare.

A stack of Granny Smith apples at the corner grocery store. Each one jet-setted here from Chile, 6,000 miles away.

All of these examples are completely *ordinary* phenomena. Yet, at the same time, oddly pleasing when you *take the time* to look at them freshly. This is just a sample to get your own creative juices flowing. See what you can see when you loosen yourself from the shackles of having to get somewhere fast. See what pops up before your eyes when your mind and heart are focused on this present moment.

Please turn off your cell phone. As you saunter, stroll, dawdle, dilly-dally, lag, loiter, lollygag, perambulate home, you're not accepting *any* calls.

# At the Supermarket:
# Avoiding the Checkout-Line Blues

On the way home, you have to hit the supermarket. Odd, isn't it? You're walking by a veritable cornucopia of food. Enough to make the less fortunate residents of Delhi or São Paulo drool. Yet you're crabby. Why?

It's the end of the day. You're beat. To make matters worse, you're hungry. Pushing a grocery cart past mounds of fresh fruit, gobs of cookies, meat positively pink in the glow of halogen lights—it all adds to your distress. The sight of all that food makes you feel hungrier. No surprise you see folk noshing on Twinkies in the aisles.

An easy remedy: Eat a nutritious snack *before* you shop. Driving or walking to the store, munch on an apple or banana or another piece of fresh fruit. Avoid scarfing down a chocolate doughnut or other sugar-loaded snack. You'll get a temporary high and then crash as you hit the checkout line. Although the fruit contains plenty of sugar, it's in a form that is absorbed by the body more slowly. You won't have to cope with the sugar blues.

Another problem with supermarkets: a superabundance of visual and audio stimulation. Obviously you can't cut down on the stress of unwanted music and incessant sales tips blasting your way. You can, however, start long, deep, slow breaths. With each inhale, imagine drawing in calm energy. With each exhale, release excess noise. Inhale and think, "Calmness." Exhale, and let go of the clamor.

Even with these remedies, by the time you get to the checkout counter, you may be cranky. Last straw: The woman in front of you insists on paying in exact change.

Her coins happen to be lurking at the bottom of her capacious pocketbook. As she digs for pennies, you fume.

Take some long, deep breaths. How about practicing seeing the other people in the line differently? It's easy to think of the people ahead of you as a hindrance. Obstacles to be removed. Rocks to be climbed over. You almost instinctively dislike them.

Start by looking at each person in a more neutral manner. No, these folks are not going to be your best friends. But can you view them less judgmentally? Give up focusing on the size of the stack of groceries in their shopping cart. Forego trying to psych out whether this one is a last-minute exchanger. Or if that one is the testy type who'll challenge the price on every item.

Now find something about each one that you actively like. Have they selected a food you happen to adore? Is she wearing a striking scarf? Do you like their shoes? Is there a cute baby in tow?

Can't find anything you like? Keep breathing and check out the next person in line. There's got to be something about this person that appeals to you. She looks (and probably is) as tired as you are. She's reading one of your favorite mystery writers. He's giggling at a silly photo in the *National Enquirer.*

Observe the person in front of you unloading groceries onto the counter without making any judgments about how fast or how slow they're doing it. Just quietly observe. Notice their hands, their fingers. The way they grasp packages of frozen food. Pretty amazing. Fingers curling and uncurling. The opposable thumb wrapping around a bag of potato chips. Eons of evolution manifested right before your eyes!

As you get closer to the cash register, turn your attention to the cashier. Look at her in a friendly way. Take a moment to see the world through *her* eyes. She's been standing on her feet since 8 A.M. Her bunions are killing her. When she gets home tonight she's going to soak her weary footsies in warm water.

Like you, she's hungry and tired. She's been shoving those bottles of applesauce past the electric scanner for hours. Back and forth, back and forth. Earlier, the scanner broke down. A customer gave her a tongue-lashing because of the delay—a delay she had no control over.

Breathe again. Thousands of shoppers have looked at this individual with unseeing eyes. Their eyes have bored right through her body and landed on the Diet Coke stacked behind her. Nobody has treated her as a unique and special human being.

What if you chatted with her today? Said casually, "Wow, it's really zooey in here today." She might not respond in any way. You may be the first customer to have spoken kindly to her in hours. She could hear the remark as a criticism. She's used to irate shoppers; she can't immediately distinguish between a neutral remark and a hostile one. Say something that makes it clear: You're on *her* side.

It doesn't really matter what you say—just as long as it's casually friendly and you look friendly as you say it. It also doesn't matter how the cashier responds. Let go of attachment to the result of your action. You reached out. It didn't cost you anything. Do this every shopping trip, and your local supermarket will be transformed. You might even look forward to your next encounter.

# Home at Last

# Postcommute Breather:
# Get a Leg Up

There's nothing like getting a load off your feet. For this one, change into comfortable clothing. Go for sweatpants and sweatshirt. Take off your shoes. Put on warm socks.

Find a room where you can be uninterrupted for five minutes. Turn off the answering machine. Turn off TV, radio, CD player. Alert your family or roommates. This is quiet time for you. You're not accepting phone calls. Neither are you up for answering any questions—shouted to you from the kitchen—regarding what type of pizza to order.

Locate a wall on which there are no prints, photos, or paintings. (Or temporarily remove them.) Find a firm surface that will be comfortable for you to lie down on. Deep pile, wall-to-wall carpeting is ideal. So is a cushioned exercise mat. Folded blankets will do. Place these up against the wall with the long end at a right angle to the wall.

This technique should be done on the floor. Tempting as it sounds, lying on your bed will not provide the delicious support your back craves. Sit sideways with your knees bent and your right hip touching the wall. This is an awkward position to get into, but don't cut any corners. Place yourself right up against the wall. Gradually lower yourself down onto the mat so you are lying on your left side, with your buttocks *touching* the wall. If your buttocks have slipped away from the wall, shift your position so that your buttocks are in contact with this surface.

Keeping your knees bent, slowly turn over onto your back. Keep your buttocks against the wall as you do this. Once on your back, extend your legs up toward the ceiling, resting the feet and legs against the wall. Be sure your buttocks are still against the wall. If they have moved away, come back into seated position and try again. It's a little tricky getting into this position, so it may take you a couple tries to get it right. There's no harm in your buttocks not touching the wall, but the relaxation benefits are much stronger if your legs are vertical and completely supported by the wall. Your hamstrings are tight? You'll want to leave a little space between the backs of your thighs and the wall. It's just fine to do so.

Lie with your arms stretched out on the floor, reaching toward your hips. Leave some space between your hips and hands, maybe five to twelve inches. Let the palms face upward. Start taking long, deep breaths. Close your eyes. If you have an eye pillow, put it over your eyes.

Feel your backbone pressing down against the floor. Imagine each vertebrae heavy, sinking down toward the floor. There are several layers of muscles that attach to your vertebrae. As the vertebrae drop down, imagine those muscles starting to relax. Let all the muscles in your back come into repose.

Keep breathing. Notice your belly rising and falling. Feel your legs and feet relaxing. After all the days' labors—the standing, walking, running, sitting—finally, your legs can be completely at ease.

Start relaxing the rest of your body. Particularly focus on places in your body where you traditionally hold tension. If it's your neck, shoulders, or back, breathe softly into these areas. Visualize the muscles expanding and relaxing. This position is so comfortable you can easily fall asleep, but please don't. Stay in the position for no more than five minutes. Then gradually come out. Have low blood pressure? Come up very slowly. Otherwise you may get dizzy.

Bonus: Many health practitioners recommend this position to help alleviate painful and unsightly varicose veins. These bulging vessels in your legs are the result of poor circulation. What happens is that blood starts to pool in the legs because weakened veins no longer efficiently return blood to the heart. Allowing gravity to pull the blood out of your legs will ease the discomfort. Relief will be further enhanced by doing gentle foot circles with your feet still up in the air.

esc

# Oh My Aching Back: Easy and Safe Stretches for a Weary Body

Congratulations! You made it through the day! Give your back the gift of five to seven minutes of easy, safe stretching.

First, relax for a minute or two in a supine position. Find a position that is comfortable for *your* back. You may feel most comfy with cushions tucked underneath your knees so your back (at waist level) is touching the floor, carpet or mat beneath you. You may want to keep adding cushions under the knees until you can no longer insert your hand between your back and the floor. If you have a tendency to be swaybacked, you may prefer to hook your legs up over an ottoman or a chair. In the ottoman version, be sure your thigh bones are vertical; otherwise the weight of your legs will put a stress on your back muscles.

Or you may feel most relaxed with your legs stretched out onto the floor with a slight arch in your lower back. Experiment. Keep making adjustments until you find the right position for your *unique* body.

Start taking long, deep, and *slow* breaths. You've been at full tilt all day. Now's the time to let yourself unwind. Let all your muscles and bones drop down and relax. Notice places in your body where you habitually carry tension. Breathe into these areas and see if you can let the muscles soften and expand.

Feeling pressed for time? You may be tempted to skip over this relaxation and proceed directly to the stretches. *Resist* this temptation. If you start stretching while your body is tight, you can injure yourself.

After a couple of minutes, roll over and come onto your hands and knees. Place your knees about hip-width apart and your hands shoulder-width apart. This one is often called the cat and dog. Your pets do a version of this all the time—it's one reason they're so relaxed!

Without forcing, gently round your back. Take a couple of deep breaths. Arch your back the way a cat arches when she's scared or posing for a Halloween card. Let your head hang, your face relax. Then let your back come into a swayback position, and look up toward the ceiling. This time your back is going to look like a swaybacked mule's. Notice if you're straining your neck when you look up. Check out your mouth. Are you tightening your lips? Relax them.

Move from an arched back to swayback several times, maybe five in each direction. Do this slowly. Very slowly. At first your back may feel stiff as a board. Take it easy. Breathe into the back muscles. Appreciate your vertebrae as you do this. They've suffered through a long day at the office, plus an exhausting commute. Your vertebrae deserve a little TLC.

If your wrists hurt, every once in a while come into a resting position where there is no weight on your hands; for example, sitting back on your heels. As you do this pose more often, your wrists will gradually become more supple and the discomfort will ease. Knees hurt? Don't do this stretch; instead substitute some of the stretches from "In the Shower."

After several rounds, come back down to lie on the floor. Rest with your knees bent and drawn up to your chest. Breathe.

Now transition back to being on your hands and knees. Let's do some circles with the hips. To start, shift your hips over to your right and then shift them over to your left. It's almost as if you were a Labrador wagging your tail side to side. Do it more slowly than the Labrador, though! Keep breathing.

Now take the hips in a full circle, to the right, then back over your heels, to the left and back to the right again. As you bring your hips and buttocks back toward your heels, feel the whole spine stretching out and lengthening. Allow the stretch to move into your arms. As your hips move toward your buttocks, let the arms lengthen and stretch toward the wall in front of you. Do this circle slowly.

When a dog wags its tail, the whole body gets into the act. The haunches wiggle side to side, the lower back sashays, even the lower ribs shift from side to side. The dog's motion is loose and floppy. He or she doesn't care about perfection.

Allow yourself to be playful. Enjoy all the points along the circumference of your circle. If the motion feels like hard work, you're trying too hard. See if you can let go of striving. Let the motion be more relaxed and fluid.

Come back to center position and breathe. Now reverse your circle and go in the opposite direction. Remember, easy does it! You're not proving anything to anybody.

Let's do one more. Again, come onto your hands and knees. Lift your right leg and reach for the wall behind you. Stretch with the entire leg, from the hip down to the toes, reaching, streeeeetching for that wall. Let go of the idea that you have to lift your leg high. Or that you're a superior person if your toes are touching the sky. Keep your leg horizontal to the floor. Take a moment to see if you can get your balance, then stretch the opposite arm toward the wall in front of you. Lengthen the whole body—deliciously, slowly—almost as if it were a piece of taffy being pulled in two directions.

Find it too hard to balance? Fine. Just do one leg at a time and then with *both* knees on the floor, lift one arm at a time. (As you practice this one, you'll gradually find it easier to balance.)

Return to lying on your back, eyes closed, facial muscles relaxed. While lying here, visualize yourself as you move into your next activity. See yourself carrying some of this calm energy with you as you prepare supper or fix a broken toy, efficiently and serenely.

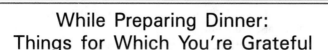

## While Preparing Dinner:
## Things for Which You're Grateful

Cooking dinner for a grumpy spouse and hungry kids? Feels like the last straw? Before starting preparations for your evening meal, think about two things that you often take for granted. This gratitude exercise will be much easier if you have already done the "Postcommute Breather." Don't have time? Don't worry, this is going to take a maximum of three to five minutes.

Sit in a chair in the Egyptian Pose. Take several long, deep breaths. For a few minutes, be grateful for your good fortune in having a stove and a ready supply of fuel. In your kitchen, all you have to do is flick your wrist. Flick. With a quick rotation of your wrist, you turn the handle on the stove. Zip! The pilot light ignites the gas. A blue burst of flame leaps up around the burner. You turn it down and prepare to sauté some garlic. Or you simply wait for the electricity to heat up the coils of the burner. In either case, the effort required is minimal: a slight twist of your wrist.

That dance of heat, whether it's provided by gas or electricity, would astonish many less fortunate people all over the planet. For them, flicks of the wrist are out of the question. The flames required for cooking depend on stooping and bending. Lifting and hauling. Gathering wood or dried dung. Imagine the trek home with prickly branches piled on top your head! Give a sigh of relief. On top of your busy day, you did not have to go out and forage for wood.

At first this gratitude exercise may irritate you. You protest, "I don't want to think of all those people who are less well-off than I am." "Enough of the planet's headaches. I have enough of my own." Yes, I know you have bills to pay. Kids who are squabbling. A boss who daily drives you nuts.

Keep breathing. Long, deep breaths. Despite your own, very real problems, your stove *is* a miracle. I use the word "miracle" advisedly. I'm not talking about divine intervention (that's for you to decide). I'm talking about one of the dictionary definitions for miracle: an extraordinary situation or accomplishment. From the average American's vantage point, the stove is distinctly ho-hum.

Seen from the perspective of a woman in Rio de Janeiro who lives in a shack without electricity or running water, your stove *is* a miracle. No doubt about it. As fantastic and unfathomable as Neil Armstrong's 1969 walk on the moon would have been to folk living in 1890.

Giving thanks today for two kitchen miracles seems like too much? If so, flex your gratitude muscles on another day. Try a Saturday or Sunday when you're less pressed for time.

Up for more gratitude? Please continue. Another flick of the wrist. You turn on the faucet. You'll use it to wash some lettuce. Again this act would be considered stunning in vast areas of the planet. The water coming out of your tap was transported via an elaborate network of pipes from the darndest places. A reservoir located hundreds of miles away, if you live in southern California. Or maybe it comes from an aquifer or your own local well.

Take a moment to appreciate the privilege you have. With the merest touch of your fingers, clear, clean water gushes out of your faucet. Sure, it may have a lingering taste of chlorine. Yes, you may choose to install a water filter or opt to buy bottled water for drinking purposes. But you have the capacity of cooking and washing with the life-giving liquid. It pours out of your faucets. In hot *and* cold versions. (If you're a person who lives in an area of serious droughts like Arizona or Texas, this exercise will really resonate with you.)

Live in an apartment building? How *did* your water get up there—high in the sky? It was piped up to you on the twenty-second floor courtesy of purring pressure pumps, gurgling pipes. Give some thanks to the sanitation engineers, architects, plumbers, laborers who helped design and build the elaborate infrastructure required to deliver water to your home or apartment.

Acknowledge the bounteousness of nature, the awe of water falling down out of the sky. Pretty amazing how a complex combination of events—wind whirling around the planet, moisture condensing off of lakes, rivers, oceans, and forests, clouds of ice crystals forming overhead, snowflakes falling out of the sky, snowflakes turning to raindrops as they get nearer the warmer earth—delivers $H_2O$ to you and yours.

Your water supply is another miracle for millions around the planet. They do without running water. They lug water in metal cans from a communal well, which may be many dusty, hot miles away. And carrying water is hard; it's heavy. Thank goodness! *You* didn't have to cap the day off slinging a pail of water onto your shoulders.

Keep breathing. You've got blessings. Many of them. Design your own personal gratitude exercises for the kitchen. The convenience of your refrigerator. The advantage of being connected to an electric grid. The beauties of organically grown, pre-washed baby carrots, which you regularly pluck from the shelves of your local supermarket.

Continue with the preparations for your dinner.

esc

# Dinner's Ready: Eating Slowly

Chances are that when you were a child, you heard the words "Don't wolf down your food," at least once. Wolves *do* wolf down their food, and they don't seem to be any the worse for wear. Eating food slowly, however, can transform the evening meal.

The first couple of times you try a *legato* meal, eat alone. If you decide to eat with a housemate or partner, tell them you'll be cutting down on the chatting.

Of course, start with some long, deep breaths. With your hands in your lap, just gaze at the nourishing edibles on the plate before you. Speaking of that plate, take the time to notice its design. Is there a decoration around the rim? Is it a swimming-pool blue or the color of a purple and pink twilight sky?

Next note the pattern and texture of the food sitting on the plate. What shade of green is the veggie? Which item looks crunchy? Which soft and creamy? Sitting here, not moving, avidly regarding your dinner, can feel like a sophisticated form of torture, up there with the rack and hanging by your thumbs.

Maybe it's a basic animal instinct imbedded in your genes: You've got to eat fast before a lion horns in on your gazelle chop. Or it could be that you grew up in a family of eternally voracious brothers. Any unguarded morsel on your plate was fair game.

Relax. Imagine you are at a museum studying one of those seventeenth-century Dutch still lifes. Each grape as translucent as glass, each apple adorned by drops of dew. A multifaceted crystal goblet reflects the ermine coat of a prosperous merchant standing nearby. Give yourself plenty of time to study the fine brushwork—of your food.

Okay. Time to pick up your cutlery. Don't get too excited—your languorous pace will continue. As you eat, observe the remarkably complicated and subtle actions you engage in to transfer food from your plate to your mouth.

Let's say you're dining on chicken, rice, and green beans. Notice how, if you're right-handed, you switch the fork into your left hand and the knife do-si-dos over into your right hand. Then you turn the fork upside down and stick it into the flesh of the chicken breast. With the other hand you bring a knife adjacent to the fork and start sawing the blade back and forth. You carefully separate a juicy tidbit from the bone. Now you maneuver the piece over toward the edge of your plate. You change hands again. The fork migrates back to your right hand; the knife reverts to your left. You spear a bite-sized portion and turn the fork right-side up. Finally, you lift the tasty morsel up to your mouth.

Usually you perform this extraordinarily complicated dance quite mechanically. But if you had one arm in a sling, you would appreciate (and be deeply frustrated by) the complex choreography of your dinner ballet. Keep breathing. Keep paying meticulous attention to the process of eating.

Now the mastication starts. Your jaw muscles, some of the strongest muscles in the body, spring into action. Teeth, a marvelous thirty-two in number, join the fray. Your incisors tear the flesh away from the fork; molars in back grind and pulverize the meat. Then muscles inside the cheeks push the food from the front of the mouth to the back. Saliva releases enzymes to help the digestive process. Your morsel of chicken (sautéed in lemon) goes down the hatch. It neatly passes through the esophagus, heading for the busy world of stomach acids and enzymes.

Notice what's happening with your hands while you're still chewing on the chicken. In your fast-paced-I'm-late life, you probably load up your fork or spoon with the next bite *before* you've finished chewing and swallowing the hunk of meat that is currently inside your mouth.

New experience: Lay down your fork *in between* mouthfuls. As you chew, put the fork down on the place mat. Yes, *down*. Let your fork languish idly on the table until the morsel in your mouth has been completely masticated. And swallowed. Only now do you raise your fork again. Whoa! Do you want to keep briskly shoveling food onto your fork and into your mouth or what?

With your next bite, examine the food itself. Say it's a string bean. Notice the long, skinny shape, the bright green color, the unique green-bean fragrance. As you put it in your mouth, observe the texture. Is it crunchy? Flaccid? Gradually let the flavor sink into the many taste buds on the tip and root of your tongue. Are there two flavors? A creamy butter taste? A sharp herb mixing with the bean flavor?

You'll want to swallow your string bean almost as soon as it hits your mouth. Borrow from the elaborate ritual wine tasters use to evaluate a fine Bordeaux. These connoisseurs stick their noses about three or four inches away from the top of the glass. They slosh the liquid from side to side and ostentatiously whiff the fragrance of the wine. Then they place their noses directly over the rim of the glass and slowly breathe in the aroma. Finally, they may take a sip of the wine, but they don't swallow. The wine is held in the mouth and savored.

Continue to saunter and dawdle through your meal, just like an old French gastronome.

# The Sweep:
# Relaxation from Toes to Head

This technique is deeply soothing. You can use it to help you drift off to sleep or simply to unwind before climbing into bed. You may want to do it in silence, or play a calming tape or CD.

Lie on your back on a carpeted floor, on a mat, or in your bed. Take the time to locate the position that works for *your* body this evening. You may feel comfy with a pillow or two tucked underneath your knees. Or you may prefer to lie with your legs stretched out flat. Start breathing deeply. Feel the belly softly rising and falling.

This is your time to let go of all the busy-ness of the day, to release worries and concerns. At first you may find you're rehashing today's conversations. Forget all those words you wanted to say to your boss and didn't. Let go of the words you *did* say and wish you hadn't. Allow your thoughts to quiet down.

Become aware of the weight of your bones. You have an astounding 206 bones in your body. You're going to let each one relax. How do you relax a bone? Technically speaking, you can't actually relax the bone itself. But by directing your attention to the bones and imagining them becoming heavier and heavier, the surrounding muscles, tendons, and ligaments will start to relax. It will feel as if your bones were dropping down. You'll start feeling more at ease.

So this is how "The Sweep" works: Your body has been resisting gravity all day long. Now you're going to surrender your body to that force. Simply let gravity take over. You'll begin at your toes and gradually work your way up to your head. As you relax different parts of your anatomy, you'll keep your mind focused on that part for a few seconds. Then you'll move on to the next part. As you're doing this, keep breathing long, deep breaths. Imagine the breath going into whichever part of the body you're currently relaxing.

Before you start, lift your head and look down at your body. Is it aligned? Lying fairly straight? If not, make any adjustments by shifting your hips, legs, or arms. Drop your head back down and now imagine all the little bones in the feet relaxing. See if you can relax each big toe. Let the arches, the soles, and the heels of each foot soften and release.

Let the ankles relax. Allow the shinbones and thighbones to become heavy. Your legs have done yeoman service lugging your body around today. Now it's their time to go off-duty. Feel the muscles in the legs becoming open and expansive. Become aware of the pelvis and hips. Let these bones become heavy. Allow the stomach muscles to soften. Feel the belly gently moving in and out with the breath.

Did you assume relaxing was one of the easiest things in the world to do? Do you now find yourself groaning, "Oh, I can't relax"? Hey, give yourself a break. You've been tense most of the day. Probably most of your life. Your 600 muscles have decades-old habits. Chronically hold tension in your neck? Your neck probably will resist relaxing. Clench your jaw whenever your boss is in sight? No surprise those wound-up muscles are not going to unwind at the drop of a hat.

Rest assured, this relaxation technique will become easier as you practice it more often. Gradually you'll learn how to relax more deeply. You'll get a sense of which muscles in your body relax more easily, and which hold on for dear life.

Continue mentally scanning up your body. Relax each vertebra. Let all the muscles in the back sink down. Feel your shoulder blades dropping down. It's almost as if they were *melting* into the surface beneath you.

Mind rushing off to plan tomorrow's conference call? Gently draw it back. Return to your breath and focus your mind on whatever part of your anatomy you've gotten to in the sequence.

Relax each rib. Let the muscles between the ribs feel more expansive and open. Breathe deeply. Relax the fingers, the wrists. Let the arms and shoulders become heavy. Allow your body to continue to sink down. Deeper and deeper. Heavier and heavier.

Let the full weight of all your bones, muscles, ligaments, organs, skin release back to be supported by the bed you're lying on. Imagine the bones so heavy that they start dropping down through the mattress, down through the wooden floor underneath you, down through the concrete foundation of the building in which you are lying. Down to the earth beneath your home. Know that you are completely supported by the earth.

Relax your neck. Take it into your consciousness: Your skull is supported by the surface beneath you. All those muscles that work to hold up your head can take a well-deserved break! Bring your attention to your face. Know that as the bones in the face relax, so will the muscles that attach to them.

Let the forehead become smooth. Allow all the worry marks to dissolve. Relax the space between the eyebrows. Relax the eyelids. Soften the muscles around the eyes and mouth. Release the jaw muscles. Be aware that as the jaw muscles untense the mouth will open slightly. Let there be a little extra space between your upper and lower teeth. Let your tongue relax. Allow it to float in your mouth.

One delicious way to practice this new skill is with a spouse, partner, or close friend. First one of you, then the other slowly and gently guides the other through the relaxation. Either read the actual text of *Serenity to Go* or go for your own version. In a soft, relaxing voice, give your partner *non-directive*, gentle cues. "Allow yourself to relax your shoulders." "Permit the neck to soften." And so forth. Allow plenty of time—at least fifteen minutes per person.

# Some Other New Harbinger Self-Help Titles

*Juicy Tomatoes*, $13.95
*Help for Hairpullers*, $13.95
*The Anxiety & Phobia Workbook, Third Edition*, $19.95
*Thinking Pregnant*, $13.95
*Rosacea*, $13.95
*Shy Bladder Syndrome*, $13.95
*The Adoption Reunion Survival Guide*, $13.95
*The Queer Parent's Primer*, $14.95
*Children of the Self-Absorbed*, $14.95
*Beyond Anxiety & Phobia*, $19.95
*The Money Mystique*, $13.95
*Toxic Coworkers*, $13.95
*The Conscious Bride*, $12.95
*The Family Recovery Guide*, $15.95
*The Assertiveness Workbook*, $14.95
*Write Your Own Prescription for Stress*, $13.95
*The Shyness and Social Anxiety Workbook*, $15.95
*The Anger Control Workbook*, $17.95
*Family Guide to Emotional Wellness*, $24.95
*Undefended Love*, $13.95
*The Great Big Book of Hope*, $15.95
*Don't Leave it to Chance*, $13.95
*Emotional Claustrophobia*, $12.95
*The Relaxation & Stress Reduction Workbook, Fifth Edition*, $19.95
*The Loneliness Workbook*, $14.95
*Thriving with Your Autoimmune Disorder*, $16.95
*Illness and the Art of Creative Self-Expression*, $13.95
*The Interstitial Cystitis Survival Guide*, $14.95
*Outbreak Alert*, $15.95
*Don't Let Your Mind Stunt Your Growth*, $10.95
*Energy Tapping*, $14.95
*Under Her Wing*, $13.95
*Self-Esteem, Third Edition*, $15.95
*Women's Sexualitites*, $15.95
*Knee Pain*, $14.95
*Helping Your Anxious Child*, $12.95
*Breaking the Bonds of Irritable Bowel Syndrome*, $14.95
*Multiple Chemical Sensitivity: A Survival Guide*, $16.95
*Dancing Naked*, $14.95
*Why Are We Still Fighting*, $15.95
*From Sabotage to Success*, $14.95
*Parkinson's Disease and the Art of Moving*, $15.95
*A Survivor's Guide to Breast Cancer*, $13.95
*Men, Women, and Prostate Cancer*, $15.95
*Make Every Session Count: Getting the Most Out of Your Brief Therapy*, $10.95
*Virtual Addiction*, $12.95
*After the Breakup*, $13.95
*Why Can't I Be the Parent I Want to Be?*, $12.95
*The Secret Message of Shame*, $13.95
*The OCD Workbook*, $18.95
*Tapping Your Inner Strength*, $13.95
*Binge No More*, $14.95
*When to Forgive*, $12.95
*Practical Dreaming*, $12.95
*Healthy Baby, Toxic World*, $15.95
*Making Hope Happen*, $14.95

Call **toll free, 1-800-748-6273,** to order. Have your Visa or Mastercard number ready. Or send a check for the titles you want to New Harbinger Publications, Inc., 5674 Shattuck Ave., Oakland, CA 94609. Include $4.50 for the first book and 75¢ for each additional book, to cover shipping and handling. (California residents please include appropriate sales tax.) Allow two to five weeks for delivery.

*Prices subject to change without notice.*